IDENTITY

JANE B. LEE

COPYRIGHT

This is a work of fiction. All names, characters, places, and events are the work of the author's imagination. Any resemblance to real person, places, or events is coincidental.

CONTENTS

FREE PREVIEW
Angel the Assassin

IDENTITY

Chapter 1

What my mother told me, way too late in our lives, confirmed what I always knew all along.

I was born as both a boy and a girl. Simple as that. Not bi anything but more of a combo identity.

Mom told me when I was four that she had made my three year-old sister a dress, and I would not give it up 'til she made one for me.

"Honey, you wore that dress for four days solid. I wouldn't let you outside." She looked me over and said, "I guess it never went away."

"Guess not!" I said as I adjusted my skirt, more out of nervousness than need.

My sister's son, his wife, and I were visiting my mother. They were there picking up Mom's old bed in exchange for a new hospital-type bed that Mom had delivered. I just dropped in; the meeting was unplanned.

I had no memory of the story she told that afternoon, but it added more than I expected to an understanding of myself, my own identity.

I do remember when I was about six, trying on my sister's dresses. Everyone that I remember in Nebraska was a girl about my age. The only other boy in the neighborhood was older and he had locked me in a shed so he could play...with me later. He was not allowed to play with me again. I do not remember that, and I do not remember him.

1

We girls played jacks, fished in the pond, jumped rope, and wandered the neighborhood. Someone had brought a horse over for us to ride. They lined four of us up on her back and took us walking up and down the street. We giggled all the way.

We all dressed alike. We wore shorts and T-shirts in the summer and long sweaters and pants in the winter. It was mostly unisex clothing. We all had the same identity.

My family moved to California that fall.

By the time I was nine, I knew I was expected to be a boy. I played my part, but I had accumulated a small female wardrobe of panties, bra, skirt and blouse. I kept them hidden under the floor of my closet. That gives credence to being in the closet. In fact, I was under it!

When the house was empty, I would dress and go about my business, homework, house work, watch TV or venture out into the back yard. I always stayed close to a backup safe place.

Around the same time, Chris moved in across the street. He was my age and part of a large, famous Hollywood family. We became playmates. Others would come and go; the neighborhood was always changing. But we were always best friends.

Chris's parents often went to Hollywood parties. We could count on them not coming home until the wee hours in the morning. I would spend the night at Chris's house when they were attending these parties.

Chris's sister, Elsbeth, had gone away to college when I just turned eleven.

Shortly after she left for college, Pat and Judy went to a Hollywood party.

I was, of course, over at Chris's house. Chris was watching TV.

I don't know how much Chris knew about my dressing as a girl at the time. I don't think he thought if it much, I think it just wasn't an issue for him anyway.

I said, "I'm going into Elsbeth's room."

"So?" He said.

I was in heaven. Her room was a literal cornucopia of girl's clothing. Dresses on the bed, thrown carelessly across chairs, literally flowing out of her closet—her bra and panties on the floor, and pouring out of her open dresser drawers. Make up, more than I had ever seen, lay in front of her mirror.

I was in heaven. Poor Elsbeth was the exact size of an eleven year-old boy! I went through her drawers, literally. I put on her panties, bra and it fit and came with its own padding, a garter belt, hose, a black skirt, and a white blouse. She had a pair of black patent leather heels; she had big feet, and they were two sizes too large for me. No matter, I slipped them on anyway.

Make up was another issue. It was all there, and I had not a clue what to do with it. Sitting in front of her mirror, I scanned the array of paints and potions. The only one I really recognized was the several tubes of lipstick. Inspecting each tube, I settled on a desert rose. I carefully lined my lips and mashed them together mimicking my mother gestures when she applied her lip stick.

Okay what now? I stood next to the door for minutes. What now? Do I step out as the person I feel like? Do I cave in to all the pressure to be the boy in my family? What now?

Taking a breath so deep I became dizzy. I opened the door. I stepped out. I clicked clacked the heels down the hall. I knew he heard me but he didn't turn around. I could see him just get a little stiff. I had known him for two years. I knew what he was thinking.

"What do you want for dinner?" I asked standing in front of the kitchen door. "Your mom left some meatloaf and boiled

3

potatoes, but I saw some hamburger. I could make that?" Chris twisted his body around on the couch. His shoulders were almost square with me. I held my breath. My body felt so heavy I could hardly bear it. It felt like minutes, hours before he spoke.

"You look nice. I'll have the hamburger," he said matter-of-factly. With that, he turned back to the TV.

I weighed about two ounces, as I floated into the kitchen.

Almost two years went by that way. Sometimes once a month, sometimes three times a month, Pat and Judy would go to a Hollywood party.

Chris and I were Ward and June Cleaver, the classic TV couple of the classic 1960s TV show, *Leave It to Beaver*. We were Chris and Lisa Cleaver. And just like the TV show we never kissed, and never touched.

I relaxed in the splendor of Elsbeth's room. Trying on clothes, and working with makeup.

The most notable thing that happened was when Chris turned thirteen. He decided that he wanted learn how to smoke! His parents smoked, his sister smoked, Ward Cleaver smoked. Chris thought he should smoke also.

We played our parts so well!

We had finished dinner, and I had cleared and washed the dishes.

The black patent leather heels by then almost fit me. Most girls were wearing their skirts above the knee or mini skirts. Mine was just above the knee, dark blue with white polka dots, underneath I wore a garter belt and hose. For panties, what I thought was sexy, was what we would now consider old lady panties. Her bras still fit. I was wearing a light-blue blouse with a small collar and white stitching. By then, I had figured out the makeup. Lipstick of course, but blush, eye liner, and eye shadow had been added. My hair was long but, not girl long. Mousse and work made it look girlish.

After almost two years since he said, "You look good," he had decided to pay me another compliments. "Hey, sexy" meant the world to me. That night as I was clearing off the coffee table, he said, "Nice ass." I blushed and shushed him.

It was ten fifteen and two hours before I had to "clean up." We heard the car in the drive and we froze. In fear, we grabbed each other hands.

"What the hell!" Said Judy.

We had stood up but did not have our wits about us, or time to run. We stood there, Chris clutching his cigarette in one hand and my hand in the other.

Pat had walked in behind Judy, his ever present pipe in hand. "What the hell! You're smoking! You're too young to start smoking! What's she doing here and who is she? How the hell am I ever going to trust you again?" Judy said, never pausing for an answer.

Chris looked at the cigarette in one hand, and me in the other.

He let go of my hand, then dropped the cigarette in the ash tray.

"Well?" She asked.

"Aah..." Was the only answer that came to his lips.

"Who are you?" Judy questioned me.

"Aah..." I echoed Chris's answer.

Pat was a bit more perceptive. He had an arm across his chest the other resting on it as he took a draw on his pipe. After a moment of silence, Pat finally said. "Is that you, Larry?"

Judy looked at me, then Pat, then Chris then back to me. The moment of recognition finally set in.

Her mouth dropped open and all she could say was a whispered "Holy shit."

What followed was humiliating, confusing, and mostly unintelligible. We were made to sit back down on the sofa. Pat was sent across the street to collect my parents.

For the next two hours, there was yelling, counseling, and a quiet but animated meeting between the parents. I was accompanied to Elsbeth's room to clean up and change.

I saw Chris only once again in my life. Our parents were in the back ground as he said goodbye. Chris was sent to a military school back east; he became a doctor.

I was required to meet with a shrink every Thursday after school: Mom drove. When I turned sixteen and had my own driver's license, Mom asked me to drive myself.

I went to the beach.

I'M CHANGING

Chapter 2

"I hate Pittsburg!" I yelled at my employees. It was Monday morning in March, at about 10:00 a.m.

About then, I chose to punch a pile of UPS boxes and turned away as they skidded across the floor.

"What the fuck!" Paula cursed as she brought her head up from behind a computer terminal.

"Damn, that hurt," I said, shaking my hand.

"It should have, don't do that again." Paula had seen that rodeo before. She turned to the two other people in the room. "Pat, Tom, time for lunch."

"But it's only ten o'clock?" Pat chimed up.

"New lunch hour," Paula declared "Now out. There is a White Castle a block away. You each got six dollars for lunch, an hour lunch. Don't come back early, don't come back late either."

As they left the shop, Paula followed me back to my desk. I flopped into my chair, throwing my arms in the air and then collapsing on my desk.

Lifting my head up, Paula noticed a gash on my lip. "Did you bite your lip again?"

"Yes, I guess," I mumbled. "Why am I in Pittsburg?"

"Because you bought a business in Pittsburg," Paula began. "And you inherited me. I'm just like that kitty cat that hangs around your front door. First, you feed it, then the kitty moves in, then the kitty tells you what to do. You can call me kitty if you like."

"Ha, you got that right pussy." I jabbed back.

"Wait, you're the pussy. I'm the kitty! Got it? So you went out last night. Still going to the wrong places, getting in fights," Paula added.

"No, I don't fight. Never have. Someone was getting all up in my face. After a while, I might have said something."

"Mouthed off!" Paula interjected.

"Maybe. Then someone punched me in the mouth, and anyway, every place in Pittsburg is the wrong place. The city deserves its name…Get it?" I tried to grin, but it turned into a grimace, and then I laughed.

Paula leaned in and said, "Honey, you still have your false eyelashes on."

"Oh shit!" I said, as I pulled them off and threw them in the trash.

Looking up Larry said. "I guess Lisa is not going to make it in Pittsburg."

I sighed deeply and fell back in my chair. "Well, when all else fails, go to the beach." I've lived that line since I was sixteen.

I thought about that for a minute as Paula chatted on. "Paula, you remember Ted Johnson?" I interrupted Paula's chatter. "He has to give out an order. This isn't difficult." As I jotted down some notes. "Call him tomorrow at nine forty-five not before because he'll be on a conference call, and at ten o'clock, he has to make a decision. Here are the three prices." Handing her the note. "Start at the top. I'll be back Monday."

I began rattling through my desk, pulling out papers and files, stopping only to type out a quick e-mail to Dr. Lora. *Please, can I use the beach house for the week?* Before packing my laptop into my ever expanding case. Paula was standing next to me, chattering away and retrieving a file here and there, asking questions and getting short answers or no answer at all. She was used to this.

My cell phone rang with an e-mail message: *Sure no problem. U know where the key is.* Three happy face emojis finished the text. Then a few second later she texted, *The gas for the stove is off, turn it on and off when U leave,* followed by a flame and wind emojis.

"You're going to the beach, right?" She had seen this show before.

"See you Monday. Don't call."

***

Friday morning, at 1:45 a.m., I received a call.

"Where are you?"

"I said don't call me. What the hell. Do you know what time it is?"

"I got a problem, help!" Paula sobbed.

"John?" Her long-term asshole boyfriend, I assumed.

"Ya, I got the matching pair to your lip and a bonus." She sobbed.

"Where are you? I'll come get you right now." I said as my feet hit the floor.

"No. No, I'm at the shop. I'm not that bad, and John's not a problem right now. Where are you? I'll come to you," Paula said.

"Oh shit! I'm at Dr. Lora's beach house on the Outer Banks. She's letting me use the place. You know it, right?" I said.

"Off the sandy road on the beach? Sure I know it." Paula gained her composure.

"Okay, just leave a note on the door for the guys to not come in and come back Monday."

Paula piped up, "Hell no. We got the order on the first number. They're working. I'm coming there, and I'll leave them instructions. I know where that place is. I can find it. I'll take a shower in the shop and clean up here. What? It's a six-hour drive?"

"About that," I said the phone went dead.

"I wish that girl would lean to say goodbye before hanging up," I said aloud to myself.

***

Paula wiped off the blood, added a little peroxide, and showered. She then wrote detailed notes: one for Tom, one for Pat, and one for both of them. Each ended with *Get it done by five. Turn on the alarm and lock the door, at five give or take a minute or two. PS Don't let John in the building for any reason.*

By now she could barely see out of her left eye. "Oh shit! This ain't good," she said aloud.

The emergency clinic took hours, including reports and additional drama. It was seven thirty in the morning before she left the clinic. Paula stopped at the Speedway for a very large cup of coffee and a full tank of gas.

Driving over to the apartment she and John had shared, she parked in view of the apartment door but far enough back not to be noticed.

John came walking out, if you could call that walking. He was holding his crotch with both hands. Paula giggled.

Paula sipped her coffee for another ten minutes. When she was sure John was gone, she rushed in and gathered up as much of her stuff as she could fit into two bags, plus a few sentimental items from long ago. She dumped those in her car. Lastly, she ran in and pulled out her Smith & Wesson .38 pistol from under the mattress and the Steven's 12-gauge pump-action shotgun and a box of shells from the closet. Putting the Smith & Wesson under her driver's seat and the shotgun and shells in the trunk, she was ready to roll.

***

Around four o'clock that afternoon, Lisa heard Paula rolling down the sand and gravel beach road. I poured her a double Irish whiskey with ice. I met her at the bottom of the stairway of the beach house; the house was built on stilts to keep it above water during hurricane season. Parking and the laundry was under the building.

I had met Dr. Lora long ago at the condo in Jersey City Heights. We shared the same love of painting and became good friends. Her getaway beach house in North Carolina was small and simple. It was on stilts next to the ocean. In front was a line of EPA-protected sea bushes, but the deck was above the tops of the bushes and allowed a great view of the Atlantic Ocean. The large deck was backed by glass sliding doors in front of a long room, the kitchen at one end, dining table in the middle, fireplace and sofa and two comfy chairs at the other end. Behind that were the two bedrooms divided by the bathroom.

I met Paula at the base of the steps next to her car. "Oh shit! You look like hell!" I said. Paula's lip was held together by one of those butterfly bandages while another one was over her left eye, which was black and red and swollen. I handed Paula her drink.

The Irish went down in one gulp. She then scooped out the ice with her hand and pressed the ice against her eye. "Ouch! That hurts so good."

Slowly, focusing with her one good eye, Paula looked me up and down. I was wearing my semipermanent hair and a long, loose white dress that buttoned down the front with the top two or three buttons open, just enough to show real cleavage, a white bra, panties, and a pair of crocheted slippers. I was wearing just light makeup. "Holy shit! You look like Dolly Parton!"

"Tits!" I said proudly. "I got tits yesterday."

"Shiner, split lip. I got them late last night" Paula said and then holding up a piece of paper "Restraining order. I got it this morning."

We hugged each other until I said, "Ouch. Tender."

"Come up onto the deck. I got more Irish and ice, and a view of the ocean."

Paula settled into a deck chair. In the kitchen, I crushed some ice cubes in a towel and grabbed the bottle of Irish on my way out to the deck.

After handing Paula the ice-filled towel and slopping more Irish into her glass, I settled into my deck chair.

"Well, are you going to let me in on what happened?" I said as I sipped my Irish.

Paula paused a minute then sipped her Irish. "I've had quite a while to think about it. Both last night and the drive over here. You know that's more than a six-hour drive? So I've had time to piece what happened together. God. It only happened last night."

She took another large swig out of her glass, and held it out for me to add some more Irish.

"When I got home last night, John was drunk again. Shit! It was already nine o'clock. He was also in a mean mood. Usually, I try to get out, but he wouldn't let me. He kept pushing me around the room, keeping me away from the door. I tried to reason with him."

"Does that mean you were yelling and screaming?" I clarified.

"Yes, on both sides for quite a while. Then he grabbed me and tried to have sex with me, to rape me."

"Holy shit! You called the cops, right? Tell me you called the cops!"

"I couldn't. He started to try and rip my clothing off. And I punched him in the face. He punched me back several time and knocked me down." She paused and sipped her Irish. "This is the good part."

"There's a good part to rape?" I nearly shouted.

"Listen! When he dropped his pants, I kicked him in the balls.

When I got up I kicked him in the balls. When he fell on the floor, I kicked him in the balls. And on the way out, I smashed his balls with his golfing trophy. I think I broke it."

"The balls or the trophy?" I was amazed. This little five-foot-two-inch, maybe a hundred-pound, woman, takes on a six foot two hundred and twenty pounder and beats the shit out of him.

"I know his balls were broken. Smashed. His fish are so smashed. If he ever has kids, they have arms coming out their head and ass. I messed him up bad."

I giggled at the thought.

"No, I think I broke his prize golf trophy." She giggled then started to laugh. "Oh, laughing hurts. Then I went to the shop and called you," she said.

"And the cops, I hope," I followed up.

"No, I called you! Remember?" She snickered.

"All you said was you had a problem with John. You didn't tell me he beat you up and tried to rape you." I defended myself. "Did you call the cops?"

"No, I went to the twenty-four-hour emergency clinic to get fixed up and checked out. They called the cops. The actual call went like this. 'Oh, Officer Roger, would you step over here?' He was right there. I guess cops hang out in the emergency clinic at night. Maybe they are assigned there. I don't know. They fixed me up. Officer Roger had me fill out some forms. He came back a few hours later with a restraining order to keep John away from me. They said they would arrest him and keep him in jail overnight when they find him and give him the restraining order. I might have to go to court."

"Good girl!" I clapped.

"Your turn," Paula said, pointing to my breasts. "Why?"

"It was time," I answered "Dr. Lora had recommended this doctor to me a long time ago, both from professional and personal experience. I had her call, and they made an appointment for me for Thursday afternoon. I spent last night in a hotel next to their offices. That's where you called me. You know the operation doesn't take long."

"Can I feel them?"

"Hell no. They hurt. And they are heavy. I got C pluses," I said proudly. "Why didn't you tell me they were so heavy?"

"Me? You're kidding. On a good day, I'm an A plus. I'm a member of the itty-bitty titty club." Looking over at me, she said, "You can't join," and laughed and then moaned, holding her eye.

"Seriously. How are you?" I asked.

"I hurt, I was a bit afraid 'til now." She held up the .38 she had under her leg. "Mad at myself for living with that shit. Mad at myself for wasting my time and money on that shit." She pauses for a moment. "Hell, now it's time to move on. Now I know everything will be all right. And you now, how are you?"

14

"I hurt, I'm scared and now that I've made a commitment to be a woman, real scared considering my past experiences. Scared about family acceptance. Scared about business acceptance. Scared that I'll never have a real relationship. Scared about having sex with men or, for that matter, women. And after all that, I'm just scared." I sipped my Irish. "But I'm happy, and I have a friend I can depend on." Reaching out for her hand.

Tears were working their way out of the corner of our eyes and beginning to find their way down our cheeks. We touched glasses. Paula said it first, "BFFs forever."

I touched her glass again; the tears were making their way down to my chin and falling in my glass, salting my Irish. I looked up, and for the first time ever, I could say, "BFFs forever."

We just sat enjoying the view not saying much, each in our own thoughts about what just happened.

We sipped our Irish; my suggestions of food went nowhere. Paula was exhausted. She reached out to hold my hand as the sun began to set behind us, throwing shadows across the sand into the ocean, darkening the waives whose lips were lined by the white phosphorescence glow of the braking wave. The horizon, like our past, was black, and as the shadows slowly crawled across the ocean, the darkening sky and sea became seamless.

Before the last bit of light left us, Paula's head moved to one side, and her eyelids slid shut. I laid the back of her deck chair flat and brought the footrest up close. I slipped a pillow under her head and covered her with a warm blanket. I lowered the awning to keep the evening dew off her. Placing a soft kiss on her forehead, I said, "We'll deal with tomorrow, tomorrow."

OH...THAT'S HOW

Chapter 3

It takes a little practice to start a fire with paper and sticks. But after four days, I was getting pretty good at it.

The beach house was a bit drafty, and March nights on the bank can be pretty nippy. The propane gas was only for the stove, which I sometime left on to warm up the place in the morning.

With Paula passed out for the night, I curled up on the sofa with my Irish and watch the flames dodge and dance, sending their light and shadows dancing across the braided rug, up the sofa then bouncing off the nearest wall, its warmth making its way into my body and soul.

My silent meditation started right here in front of this fireplace Monday night. I didn't try to think too much on the six-plus-hour drive down from Pittsburg. I had some pretty specific ideas that flopped around in my brain. Like fish in the bottom of a boat, every time you think you got a hold on it, it slips out of your hands!

Monday night on my way in, I stopped at Tim's Pizza, a little place just before I turn on to the sand and gravel road for the two-mile drive down the island to Dr. Lora's beach house. Tim made great New York–style pizza.

After settling in, I enjoyed my pizza and a glass of cheap red wine on the deck. I was all wrapped up against the night air. Then I spent the better part of an hour getting a fire going. The sticks were the key to getting the fire going quickly. It took me most of an hour to figure that one out.

After settling in with a warm fire going, I could start to put things together. I asked myself, *How did I get to Pittsburg?* That was quickly followed by *and what do I do now?* Then just as quickly, and *who do I really want to be?*

I started by questioning my childhood, going all the way back to six, when I first remember wearing my sister's dresses. I decided this would take forever, and I would just be going over well-trodden ground, fertilized by hours of therapy. *No, I had to narrow the field to a more specific time frame.*

First marriage? No, too long ago. And, Ashley didn't allow me to cross-dress. I had to have a secret suitcase for business trips only.

Second marriage? Cross-dressing was allowed. Jessie even encouraged it. But I couldn't leave the house until the coast was clear. Nobody could know. That finally led to me being firmly encouraged to move out. She even packed my bags for me.

Which brought me to my next stop, New York City. Actually, New Jersey. I moved into Jersey City Heights for half the price of living in New York City, and I had a fabulous view of Manhattan. I moved in as Lisa. My landlord and neighbors only knew me a Lisa. Also, the butcher, baker, and liquor store owner only knew me as Lisa.

I got hit on a lot. I even went to a couple of dinners with men I had met. I made friends with the women in the building. I had almost no problems 'til Lisa tried to get a job. Lisa was not employable.

So the only thing I could do was find a job as the Larry in me. In fact, I found a good paying sales job in Roseland, New Jersey, far enough away so that I would not expect my coworkers to show their faces in the neighborhood yet close enough to both work and the airport that I wasn't spending hours driving.

Then came the juggling, trying to keep Larry to a minimum in the Heights and Lisa out of Roseland. What became a later problem was several cross-gender, gender-crossing incidences.

Coming home one Wednesday night at about ten thirty after a long trip and a flight that seemed to take forever, I was too tired to lug both Lisa's and Larry's luggage plus my briefcase up five flights of steps, so I took the elevator.

On the second floor, the elevator stopped. *Shit*, I didn't need that. Mary Beth Jones stepped in. The building only had twenty-two apartments. Everyone knew everyone, and we all looked out for each other. Strangers were always questioned.

"Hi. Who are you?" Mary asked right off. At eighty-two, she felt like she didn't have time for unnecessary formalities.

"Larry." I said in the most male voice I could muster.

"Where are you going at this time of night?" Mary demanded. Part of the neighbor code is to know who was who and who was staying with who.

"Lisa Wynn's apartment. I'm her cousin. She said I could stay here."

"Well, Lisa's not here!" Mary continued her interrogation.

"I know. She's in Dallas, I think," I countered.

"She's not here much anymore..." Mary's voice trailed off.

"We both have been traveling a lot lately, so we decided to share apartments. Seemed to make sense." I laid the groundwork.

I decided to take control of the situation. "And what's your name?"

"Mary Beth Jones, 4B. Welcome, Larry. You look a lot like your cousin. Father's side, I bet."

"How perceptive." I said, deciding to finish the background story. "I live in Atlanta. I am usually at home during the weekends. I've got a number of clients here and in New York City, so I guess I'll be here on and off for a while."

"I see," Mary said. I knew she would spread the word, and I could ride the elevator whenever I wanted.

So then Larry could visit a lot, and Lisa bought the groceries and wine. That wasn't really how I wanted to live my life, so I started taking Lisa on extended business trips.

Within less than a year, I had become so comfortable with Lisa, I had to remind myself that Larry had a job, which brings me to my next and even larger problem. One Sunday afternoon, I left for Newark airport as Lisa and didn't even think about it until I walked into the terminal. *Holy shit*, I thought to myself. *You've done it this time Lisa, just how am I going to get out of this? I can't. I'll just have to do it! Suck it up girl.*

The TSA pre pass line was short on Sunday afternoons, so it didn't take long for me to get to the agent. *First problem, ID.* I handed my driver's license to the seated TSA agent, a rather large man in his late fifties, I guessed. He looked at Larry's driver license. He held it up, comparing me to the picture, and said loudly "Is this you? Larry Wynn?"

"Yes." It was a very quiet yes as I leaned in toward the agent.

"What?" He asked even louder "Are you Larry Wynn or not."

"Yes, that's me," I said in an even female voice. "Is there a problem?"

"No problem, Mr. Larry Wynn. Next."

Placing my purse and carry-on on the belt to be scanned, I then was directed to the body scanning booth.

"Please step in. Place your hands over your head." I stood quietly as the bar moved back and forth.

As I stepped out on the other side, I was informed by another TSA agent, "OK. You have been randomly selected for further inspection."

"Oh really, randomly?" I asked.

"Yes, really, Mr. Larry Wynn. Please come this way." He led me off to a small room near the security center. "Please step into this room for a private inspection."

The male TSA agent stepped in with me. My hand hit the door before it could close.

"Mr. Larry Wynn, you could be arrested and rejected from the airport for refusing inspection."

"I'm not refusing. I'm requesting a female agent also be present. I think that is a valid, reasonable, and legal request."

A full thirty seconds passed as we looked at each other. I'm sure he had not read his manual, and I wasn't sure if it was a legal request or not. But he thought it might have been a legal request.

"Martha," he called out, "would you join us, please?"

I stood with my arms out and legs apart. The male agent patted down the lower part of my body and the female the upper parts.

"Are those real? I mean are they prosthetics?" She asked, gesturing toward my bust.

"Yes, prosthetics," I answered, looking her directly in the eye. "May I see one?"

"Left or right?" I asked without skipping a beat and still holding eye contact as she flinched.

"Either," she said, looking away. I handed her my left breast.

She took it into her latex gloved hands.

"I just need to scan it for explosives. I'll be right back," she said, leaving the room with the male agent.

Ten minutes later, she returned my left breast. Explosive free, I was allowed into the boarding area just in time to watch my flight take off without me.

Well, Atlanta. There is a flight every hour or so," I thought and walked into the sky club to get re booked on the next flight and ordered a scotch, a much needed scotch.

The female counter person smiled as I walked up. "Can I help you, miss?" I explained I was detained by TSA for further inspection and missed my flight to Atlanta. I handed her a note from TSA that I had demanded and my ticket.

She looked at it and said, "No problem, Miss. Happens all the time," as she tapped away on her computer.

"Great, I can get you on a flight for Atlanta, leaving in about an hour, and I can get you up graded to first, Miss Wynn. Window or aisle?"

Therein lay the difference between government employees and company employees, both of whom serve the public.

Did I forget I was Lisa or, thinking back, it might have not been just because I forgot? I might have wanted to forget.

However, that wasn't the end of the Newark TSA encounter. Someone from the company or someone who knew someone from the company was present. Probably at the ID inspection was where they got me. The word got back to the company.

I was traveling for my customary two weeks. When I got back, it was subtle at first. First, my assignments were changed. Instead of office buildings, I got steel mills or chemical plants. At the same time, I was requested to spend more time in the office and no more weekend travel.

Identity

First the rubbers and birth control pills showed up on my desk to snickers from the office staff. My e-mail was full of drag queens, dogs dressed as drag queens, and increasingly rude pictures of gays and lesbians.

Complaints to management were met with blank faces. I was promised that things would change, and they would get to the bottom of it. After their office door closed behind me, I heard, "Bottom of it, get it?" And giggles.

If someone can rape a person without even touching them, that's how I felt.

I had a little inheritance set aside. I decided to use it. I scanned the web for weeks for the right business for sale.

I found a small business in Pittsburg. It met my parameters for type of business and was reasonably priced. I called, introduced myself, and we exchanged nondisclosure agreements. I requested a meeting for the following Monday.

The following Monday, Larry walked in, asking for Sonia. "I'm Paula. May I ask your business?" Paula always ran interference for Sonia. She directed Larry to the back desk.

Sonia was surprisingly frail, yet beautiful for any age.

I understood her and her me in less than a minute. We talked business.

"Sonia, we will make a deal. Just one thing."

"And that is?" Sonia asked.

"Have dinner with me tonight, and we'll work out the details."

A smile came across her face. "My pleasure."

We met at seven at a very nice restaurant. I tried to make some light conversation at first.

Sonia came right to the point. "My husband started the business, but after just two years, he passed away. We have no kids and no family, so I had to run the business for the last eight years." She paused to take a sip of her wine and think for a minute. "I'm not very good at it. Paula does most of the work. I just manage the accounts."

I sipped my wine. I have learned when someone has something to tell you. Let them.

Sonia looked me in the eye. "Now, honey, I've got cancer. Give me enough money for at least three years in Florida. Please."

"Sonia, do you know how much that will cost?" I asked.

"About $75,000 a year," she said flatly.

I thought for a few minutes, sipping my wine. Dinner was served. We sat quietly.

"Sonia, how about this. Instead of me giving you $225,000 or negotiating a more realistic price, I'll pay you $75,000 a year for the rest of your life."

She looked at me, thinking then said, "I don't even know how to write that up."

"Neither do I. That's what attorneys are for." I followed up, "Deal?"

Sonia weighed her options. "Deal." We sealed the deal with a clink of the wine glasses. They rang true and pure.

Oh, that's how I got to Pittsburg!

CHICAGO INC.

Chapter 4

The fire had finally given up and gave the house over to the morning chill. It was not quite yet dawn.

No matter how tightly I balled myself up on the sofa, the chill still invaded my space. Giving up, I pulled the light blanket over my shoulders. First things first, I walked over to the open kitchen, and I turned all four burners on the stove full blast. That not only heated the room but also provided a faint light in the dark room.

Second thing, go to the bathroom. Third thing, change into something warmer and get out of this stale dress. As I entered my bedroom, I remembered that it had a small electric heater. The room was warm and comfortable. "Why the hell did I fall asleep on the sofa?" I questioned myself. "Oh yes, I was thinking or was it more like remembering how I got to this place at this time and planning where I'm going next."

I unbuttoned my dress and let it fall to the floor. A warm robe and fuzzy slippers replaced my dress. My bra was always on. The doctor required me to wear a bra for the next few months. I guess the bra was needed to keep my new puppy noses warm and cozy.

The coffee pot was an old fashion percolator. It was the same kind as my grandparents kept on their stove and had just about as many dents. I measured the coffee into the metal basket, one spoon for each cup; that's eight, and one for the pot, nine in total. I placed it on one of the burners and turned the fire down a bit. In a few minutes, I would hear the *perk, perk* as the water started to hit the glass cap.

I went about putting bread in the toaster and retrieving butter and raspberry jam from the fridge. By the time that was ready, so was the coffee.

I poured a cup for Paula and me. Paula had suckered me into putting cream in my coffee; since then, I couldn't drink coffee without cream.

On the deck, Paula was nowhere to be seen. She had pulled the heavy blanket up over her head and curled into the fetal position.

The morning sun was just announcing itself, poking yellow rays into the clouds over the ocean. Having conquered the clouds, the not yet fully-risen sun began chucking yellow rays our way.

I pulled back the blanket, exposing the top of Paula's head. "I feel like shit" came drifting up from under the blanket. Paula slowly unfolded herself, saying, "I smell coffee." She gradually sat up, stretching and pulling the warm blanket around herself. One hand reached out for her coffee.

"Owe! That hurts," Paula said as she took her first sip of coffee, forgetting about her split lip. Touching her swollen lip then the cut above her black eye. "Did you get the number of that bus?"

"The bus's name was John, and a train ran over his balls, remember?" I told her.

We both laughed until Paula said, touching her lip then forehead, "Oh shit. Don't make me laugh, please."

"Breakfast is ready, and the house is probably warm by now," I said as I stood and led the way into the house and over to the one wooden table. The table was in the middle of the room and served as an all-purpose table with six chairs, three on either side.

Paula thought for a few minutes as I served up the breakfast toast. "Well, I guess I'll have to find a new place to live?"

I walked silently over to the door. Next to the door were several hooks for keys. I separated my apartment key from the nest of keys on my key ring. I dropped my apartment key on the table in front of her.

Paula looked up at me.

"I'm not going to need it anymore," I said.

Paula was puzzled and asked, "What? What do you mean? What's up?"

"Paula, I made some big decisions this week."

"I can see that, C-plus cup decisions," she said, referring to my new breasts.

"Actually, that's part of it, but not all of it." I sat down, looking at Paula over the rim of my coffee cup. "The business is not going to make it in Pittsburg." I watch for Paula's reaction.

Paula put down her cup of coffee; placing both arms on the table and folding her hands, she leaned forward and looked me directly in the eye, she said, "So what are you going to do about it?"

"Actually, I've been working on that all week." Looking down at my new breasts, I said, "Except for Thursday noon and some of Friday." I chuckled.

"I've been calling banks and working on a SBA loan. I've also been looking around at different cities. Chicago is better suited for a business like ours. It has a good workforce. O'Hare airport is central to travel. And lots of potential business in and around Chicago for our kind of product."

"Chicago," Paula said

"Well, more specifically, Highland Park or Evanston." I paused for effect.

"Evanston, Highland Park," Paula repeated after me.

"We can do more business there in a week than we can do here in a month. Hell, probably a year," I said.

"How you going to do that? What's going to happen to the guys? Hell, what going to happen to me? How are you going to pull off the move?" Paula asked.

I answered, "First, the guys have roots here and families. I'll offer for them to come with us, but they won't move. Second, next week, I'll close on the loan, get a place, and start selling."

"And how are you going to do all that with those C-plus puppies you adopted?" Paula asked.

"Larry Lee Wynn is no more! Lisa Lee Wynn is taking over the business," I said firmly. Then again I paused, looking Paula in the eye. "Along with my new partner with 20 percent ownership. Paula."

Paula leaned in further, looking me in the eye. She said, "Really?"

"Serious," I answered, and Paula knew by the tone of my voice I was serious.

Paula did not move or say anything for several minutes. I knew to always let the buyer close the deal.

Paula leaned back and, slapping the table with both hand palms down, said, "What the hell. I have no reason to stay in bloody Pittsburg. Let's move to...where was that?"

"Highland Park or Evanston, Illinois," I said with a smile. We both got up and rushed around the table and hugged each other, which was a much bigger commitment than shaking hands.

The rest of Saturday and all of Sunday was filled with plans, ideas, and arguments, all leading to a concise plan, one that we both could believe in.

***

Identity

On Monday, we cleaned the house and stocked the cupboard with two cases of wine and two bottles of Irish. I called Dr. Lora and thanked her profusely for the use of her beach house and spent the next thirty minutes filling her in on my new C pluses and my new plans for the business. She wished me luck and promised to visit on her next trip to Chicago.

On Monday evening, Paula made herself at home in my, now her apartment. She helped me pack as much stuff as possible in to bags and boxes. I was moving, no matter what.

***

Tuesday morning after breakfast, I was preparing for the airport. I was all packed up in a large carry-on and two large bags, one for shoes and the other for clothing.

I called Paula into my bedroom.

"Can you help me with this thing?" I had started wrapping an Ace bandage around my chest.

"What the hell? Just get your dress on and let's go," she demanded.

"I can't. Lisa can't fly. Well, she can. It's just that TSA is a pain in the ass and will guarantee that Lisa will miss her flight. So, Larry," I said, holding out the bigger end of the Ace roll.

"What happened, sweetie?" Paul asked.

"I'll tell you on the way to the airport. Now please wrap me, tight."

Just off the airplane at O'Hare airport, I made my way to the nearest handicap restroom. Larry walked in Lisa walked out. Lisa could handle anything else, cabs, hotels, banks, and landlords. And so, alone, Lisa entered the world.

Chapter 5

Lisa made a deal at the Marriott Suites, just one block off of Michigan Avenue and one block north of the Handcock Towers for a little more than $700 a week.

Wearing her favorite suit with the skirt just above the knees and showing ample cleavage, she closed on the bank deal on Thursday. On Monday, she closed on a lease in Highland Park with an option to expand. On Tuesday, she saw an attorney for business and another for changing her sexual identification. The first went great; the second was disappointing. Wednesday, Thursday, and Friday, Lisa was on the phone, making appointments.

Within three weeks, she had closed enough deals to guarantee the next year's income at ten times her best year in Pittsburg. It turned out that Lisa was a far more successful salesperson than Larry ever was, and he was good. Cleavage and legs got Lisa in the door; ability got her the order.

In less than two months, the transfer was complete.

Paula moved in with Lisa in a nice condo, just three blocks from Lake Michigan. It had two stories, three bedrooms that are better described as two bedrooms and an office, two bathrooms, and best of all, a small patio with a barbecue.

For the two of them, Saturdays were still working days. They call Saturday the bonus day. They joked about it. The habit on Saturday became to work from nine in the morning to four in the afternoon then head out to the Arrow Restaurant and Bar for wine and dinner. The Arrow was a nice place, close to their apartment and far enough from work not to be disturbed by employees.

Eric, the bartender, soon learned what they drank, where they wanted to sit, and most of all, never ever interrupt an argument. Once he tried to suggest a solution, that didn't go well. Eric was welcomed into most other conversations. He was a little gun shy at first but learned that those two friends wanted him as a friend as well.

One of the other regulars was Dave, a builder whose offices was not far from Lisa and Paula's growing shop. After a few Saturdays, Dave got Eric to introduce him to Lisa and Paula.

"I'm Dave" was all he had to say and flashed that incredible smile. That clanging sound I heard was Paula's guard falling to the floor. The walls she had built up since John were melted with just one smile.

The following Wednesday, Dave showed up at the shop. Paula met him at the door. A few minutes later, she came back to my desk. "Mind if I take an early lunch?" Paula asked excitedly.

Looking over her shoulder at Dave, I asked, "And how long do you need?"

"An hour…Depends on how things go. Maybe two if it goes well." She was glowing.

It was a two-and-a-half-hour lunch. On Saturday, Dave met us at the Arrow. On Sunday, they went to the horse track. Paula came home late.

A few weeks later, we finally found a good bookkeeper. She had worked at a bank and had very good skills. Anna had not really worked in a while and had been fired from the one job she was able to land after only a few days. We both interviewed her. She had worked at the bank since graduating from high school, then she took accounting courses to improve herself and worked into a better position. Then she met Frank and fell deeply in love. Anna quit her job to marry Frank. Frank died two years later in a traffic accident. Telling us her story, tears came to her eyes. We offered her a tissue and hired her.

Now we didn't have to work Saturdays.

***

One Saturday morning, over breakfast coffee, Paula announced, "Dave asked me to move in with him."

"Really." I was not shocked.

"Yep. But it's only been four months. It's too early," she said, looking to me for direction.

"Well, my first marriage was just five months from first date to the altar," I said. "And look how that worked out. You had better wait."

Two months later, I received a phone call from my attorney. "Lisa, can you be in the courthouse Thursday next? I think the judge has some good news for you."

"Oh God, yes. Great, yes, yes," I stammered on.

It had taken almost a full year and several thousand dollars. I had to have six psychological sessions ordered by the court to determine if I would be a good woman.

I called Paula into my office. "We're taking next Thursday off. Saturday, we're going to Michigan Avenue."

I was pacing and talking very fast. "I need a new business suit, a new blouse and bra, and everything and...oh and shoes and a purse, and I got to get my hair done. Nails. I need new nails and maybe something else...I don't know."

"Stop. Stop. Stop. What the hell is going on?" Paula tried to slow me down.

"Got a call from my attorney," I said with both hands in front of me and tears forming in my eyes.

"Oh, I get it. You're getting admitted to the female sex, right?"

"Yes." I said now with tears streaming down my cheeks.

Paula grabbed me and gave me a hug.

"Congratulations, girl." And Paula gave me another hug.

***

On Thursday, we were at the courthouse closer to nine than ten. We sat on the wooden benches that lined the hallways of the courthouse. We amused ourselves, trying to guess what offense various characters in the hallway might be there for.

My attorney walked up to us just after ten. "The judge wants to see you in her chambers." Pointing to Paula "You can come along too."

The judge's chambers were enormous. It had to be just to hold her enormous desk. We were not invited to sit. We stood in front of the desk. Paula stood to my left, and my attorney to my right. Behind the judge was a clerk holding some papers. I could not decide what to do with my hands. First, I put them behind me then in front of me and finally at my sides.

The judge was reading some documents. She looked up after more than a minute, a long quiet minute.

"So, Lisa, I have read your file." Sitting back, taking off her glasses. "Are you ready to do this thing?"

"Absolutely," I answered quickly.

"Any last questions?" She followed up.

"No, I think I have gone over everything. I read the material. I have had my psychological sessions. I'm committed. I made my decisions long ago. I'm ready," I said as firmly as I could in as feminine voice as possible.

"OK then." As she signed some papers in front of her and handed them to the clerk next to her to notarize. "I now pronounce you Lisa Lee Wynn. Welcome to the female gender."

I said thank you lots of times. I collected my papers and hugged Paula and my attorney.

On my way out of the judge's chambers, the judge called me back. "By the way, Lisa, you look quite lovely."

In the hallway, the attorney excused himself to attend to another client.

Paula hugged me again and repeated the judge. "You're lovely, you have been judged lovely by a real judge."

"Can I go get my new driver's license now? Please?" I begged.

"Hell no! We would be hours and hours sitting there. It's after ten, and every teen in the country is trying to get their driver's license. It will be packed. We'll go first thing in the morning. We'll be the first ones in line. Maybe," Paula promised. "And don't wear heels!"

***

By the time we got our car and fought our way through the traffic and up the Edens Freeway, it was noon. We called Dave, and we all met at the Arrow. We toasted me. We eventually got around to a late lunch.

We decided to have a small dinner party on Saturday to celebrate my newfound and legal identity. Just a small party, only Dave, Paula, Anna and myself.

Over the last few months, Paula and I had become quite attached to our Anna. She had few, if any, friends and was haunted by bouts of depression. As the bookkeeper and assistant, she knew everything and was included in many meetings. As an employee, she was trustworthy and loyal. As a person, she was sweet and loving.

At first, the depression episodes were difficult to figure out how to handle. We tried talking to her to try and bring her out of her depression. That seemed only to make it worse. We tried to distract her with a project or extra work. That didn't work either. Finally, we just had her lay down on the sofa we had placed in the ladies' room. That worked, and it usually took less than ten minutes for her to come out her sweet self.

***

On Friday morning, I collected my new driver's license for Lisa Lee Wynn with my new photo.

On Saturday morning, over coffee, Paula said, "Serious now."

"Stop. You can't say that. That's my line. Come up with your own line," I said.

Paula gave me the "what?" look. "Okay, how about 'listen up'?" she asked.

"Good. And that's more like you. So what?"

"I'm moving in with Dave," she announced, looking for my reaction.

I took a deep breath and looked away. Turning back. "Sweetie, I'm going to miss your cleaning up around here. But I'm going to miss your sweet face every morning even more. But you have to follow your heart. Most important, follow your heart."

"I haven't told him yet. If it's okay, I want to announce it tonight." Paula waited for my reaction.

"I'm going to miss you so much," I said as she reached across the table for my hand.

"Honey, it's going to be all right. We work together. We party together, and we're BFFs, remember? Don't worry," Paula said.

The dinner party came off just fine. I cooked tuna on the grill and asparagus sautéed with bacon and garlic. Rice done with mushrooms and onions finished off the dish. After lots of wine and with the plates removed from the table, we brought out a small bottle of port. We all sat around, sipping the last of our port.

Paula put her hand on Dave's arm. "What was that again? That thing you have been asking me to do for weeks or months?"

Dave got a big grin on his face. "Princess, I don't think they want to know about our sex life."

"No silly." Paula slapped Dave's arm.

"Oh, you mean will you move in with me." Dave smiled.

"No," Paula said then slowly said. "Ask me properly."

Dave stood and backed out his chair. Kneeling on one knee, he took Paula's hand. "Paula, will you move in with me?"

"Yes." And then lots of kisses and hugs.

More wine was poured and the glasses chimed in their acceptance. Dave and Paula left shortly after that. We saw them to the door. Anna turned and retreated to the living room sofa. I wasn't quite sure why she was hanging around. I retrieved our wine glass and a bottle of merlot wine and sat next to her. I wasn't sure if she was going into one of her now not-so-frequent depressions. I was concerned.

"I want to thank you so much for hiring me and being my friend, and I'm so happy for you," she said, taking my hand.

"Honey, are you okay?" I asked, squeezing her hand.

"Sometimes it hurts. I miss Frank so much. I haven't dated. I don't know how." The tears were starting to form in her eyes. "What am I going to do?" The tears started to run and turned into sobs. "I'm so lonely."

I moved closer and put her head on my chest and my arm around her. It wasn't depression; it was a breakdown.

"Paula and Dave seem so happy," she said. "Why can't I find someone and be happy?"

"Let it out. Just let it out." I comforted her.

She sobbed on for a few minutes and then grew quiet and a little restful. In about fifteen minutes, she straightened up. The drink napkins became handy tear caddies.

"I'm just lonely," she said.

"I understand," I answered.

Looking at me, she said, "Do you want to know something?" Not waiting for an answer, she went on. "In high school, I had a lesbian lover. I never told Frank."

Oh, where is this going? I thought.

"I was a sophomore, and she was a senior. Pat, Patricia, was tall and beautiful. I was a virgin of, course, but the relationship only lasted three months. Then she found someone else."

"Okay," I said, wondering, *what am I supposed to do with this information?*

"I only told you because... Oh, never mind," she said as she sighed and fell back.

"Go ahead. Say it. We can't have it hanging in the air for God knows how long. Just say what you're thinking," I said.

Anna gathered up her courage. "I only told you because, now that you're a woman, a very beautiful woman. If you wanted to you know, be with me; I'd be happy to...you know."

"Oh, Anna." I petted her hair and reached for her hand. I chose my words very carefully. "Anna, you are so beautiful and so young. You're smart and sensitive and loving. You're a treasure for anyone."

I thought for a minute. "I'm where you are. I haven't dated in years either. And I would be with you in a heartbeat. But."

"But?" Anna repeated after me.

"Yes...but for two things," I continued. "One, you work for me. I can't do that. I can't have an affair with you. And I could not do just one night. It never works, and it only leads to bad things."

"But you and Paula. I thought you and Paula," Anna started.

I put my hand up. "Paula and I are sisters. We love each other and would do anything for each other. But we never ever got close to having sex."

"Oh," Anna said, looking away.

"Second. Do you even know if you want a man or a woman for a lover?" I questioned her.

"I don't really know. I had that wonderful experience with Patricia. Never anything like it. But then, I started dating men. It was kind of expected, I guess. But I keep thinking back. I don't know."

"Guess what? I don't know either. Also, I haven't dated in such a long time either." We both sipped our wine.

"It's not just the sex. God knows, I could use some," I said. "Me too," Anna joined in.

"It's having somebody. A lover. Right now, it's even harder on us when we see how happy Paula is," I noted. "They are a reminder of our being just one."

We both sat for a few minutes, sipping our wine.

"I got an idea," I said. "Now that Paula's got Dave, I'm not going to see her as much."

"So?" Anna wasn't following.

"So let's double date! We both can go out with guys. Then women. Then maybe mix it up a bit. It's a double date, so we can help each other. Help keep us from making mistakes. Especially mistakes we make when we're horny."

The light was going on in Anna's eyes.

"This way, we can figure out if we're lesbians or not. And I won't have to fire you. You're so sweet and lovely. I would hate to lose you over this," I said.

"Okay. Just how are we going to do that? Get two guys or two women to go out on a double date with us." Anna was all in now.

"Dating service," I said. "I'll find one. We'll go in, and we'll be out on a date by Friday. What can it hurt? And we might even get laid."

***

We took our lunch hour on Monday; it turned into a two-hour lunch, and we visited a dating service. We filled out the paperwork and answered their question. The one question that they hung up on was, "What kind of men do you want to double date with?"

"Well,"—we looked at each other—"we would like to start dating women. Professional women around our age."

"Okay." She did hesitate a bit. "We have a number of clients that are lesbians."

"Not just that." We again looked at each other. "Or men."

At that, she looked up with a confused look on her face. Hands and fingers stopped in midair.

Identity

"We're trying to find out if we're lesbians or not," Anna answered. "You don't know by now?" The counselor asked, incredulously.

"Well. It's this way." I began telling her our stories.

Chapter 6

The new driver's license worked wonders at TSA. Not only that, but renting a car was a breeze. Hotels were no longer a guessing game to see if my fake transgender ID would work. Best of all, I was pulled over doing seventy-six in a sixty-five-mile-an-hour zone. The cop asked for my license and called it in to check on my driving record. I had no tickets as Lisa. He then stood by the car, looking down my blouse, chatting. He finishing off by saying, "Okay, miss, just hold it down." My driver's license was my key to the world, or so I thought.

Back in the office a few days later. I hung up the phone. I waved Paula into my office and tried to put some kind of list together. "Paula, we got an opening. Somebody dropped out of the Singapore conference at the last minute. They have an opening, and I took it." I looked up as I told her. The conference was hosted by the US State Department and the US Chamber of Conference. It was a chance for US manufactures like our little company to present themselves to Asian companies that could likely use our services. Even better, the government was picking up our conference fees and providing us with a daily per diem.

"Yahoo!" Paula boxed the air.

"I just got the flight reservations. I leave tomorrow morning at 6:12 a.m. Help me get things packed. Where are my business cards? I'll need a couple of hundred, I hope?"

"Okay, I'll round up some brochures and resumes. Maybe some of those pictures I took. I got a file of them. What else?" Paula was ahead of my list.

43

"It's nearly four. I need to pack. Come home with me and help me pack. Oh, and please, if you don't mind too much, call Dave and say you're staying the night to help me?" I begged.

"No problem. Get your things together, but don't put them in your bag. I want to double check." On the way out my door, Paula called Anna in to help me.

While we were gathering things up, Anna elbowed me.

"What did you think of Carole?"

We had been double dating with people from the escort service for about two or three times a month for the last three months. The last two dates were with women. We both got called several times for second more private dates by both the men and women. Anna went on a few both with men and women. I never accepted a second date. I had lots of excuses.

"Carole? Are you sure? I liked Pam a lot better." Anna's preference for women had become obvious over the last few dates.

"Yes, but Pam was your date. I can't cut in," Anna said.

"Yes, you can, and Pam was a lot more interested in you than me. Tell you what." As I fished around in my purse for a small card case. "Here it is" As I handed her a card. "You call her."

"I can't. I'm the feminine one, you know," she said.

"Oh please. You both are so feminine that if you don't make a move, neither one of you will. Do you want that? Call. Call tonight," I ordered.

I was very pleased with the progress our baby sister was making. Paula walked in as Anna was walking out. "Look." Anna held the card up.

"Carole?" Paula asked.

"No, Pam," Anna called back.

Paula looked to God for guidance and shook her head. "At least she's happy. Did you notice? No more depression swings. Now, I'll hand things to you, and you pack them away."

We picked up Chinese dinners to go as we headed to my house. We settled in my bedroom and began filling a carry-on and a large suitcase.

"It's going to be hot. So light stuff only. Except maybe for the flight. It can get a little chilly on airplanes sometimes." Blouses, skirts, shoes, panties, bras, dresses makeup kits all started to get gobbled up by the hungry suitcase and carry-on.

"Got your passport? Be sure you got your..." Paula saw my face drain white. "You don't have one do you?"

"Shit." I sat on the side of the bed, my head in my hands. "No way. Shit."

Paula sat on the side of the bed with me and put her arm around me, her head against mine. "I hate to ask this. But does Larry have a current passport?"

I looked over at her. "Yes." I sighed "I'll get it and some of his clothes."

***

The next morning, wrapped in an Ace bandage, we left for the airport, Larry's passport in my pocket. I didn't bother with a wallet, just money and credit cards wrapped in their own bandage, a rubber band.

Chicago, Japan then Singapore takes more than thirty hours. Finally, on the ground in Singapore, I placed my bags on the inspection line.

"Is this your bag?" The uniformed customs agent asked.

"Yes," I answered.

"Who are you traveling with to Singapore?"

"Just me," I said with a smile, my last smile for a while.

"Please step over here." Gesturing to a small room.

The interrogation room had a table, two chairs, and no windows. We were joined shortly by another uniformed agent, Emily by her name tag.

Emily opened my suitcase and spread parts of it across the table. "Are these items yours?" Gesturing to my female clothing and wigs.

"Yes," I slowly said.

The first agent, his name badge identified him as Paul, said, "Let's see what we have here," gesturing to Emily to go through my stuff.

Emily opened up my makeup case and examined it more closely, even smelling my perfume bottle. She slowly unpacked the rest of my suitcase, placing my dresses, skirts, and blouses neatly on the table. She held up my bras by the straps and placed them next to my panties on the table.

Finally satisfied that I wasn't smuggling any guns, gum, or other contraband into Singapore, Paul, the one who appeared to be in charge, turned to me and said, "Male prostitution is not legal in Singapore."

"What? I'm not a prostitute!" I followed that up with an explanation of my business and my reasons for being in Singapore.

To which he replied, "MALE prostitution is not legal in Singapore," with an emphasis on MALE.

This had me assuming that female prostitution, if not legal, was at least acceptable.

"I am NOT a prostitute." I emphasized NOT.

Paul went on to explain just where on Orchard Road the male prostitutes, some of whom dressed as women, gathered usually between the hours of 4:00 p.m. and 10:00 p.m. Also, he told me why it was important to move on by 10:00 p.m. That's when the park was cleared out by the authorities.

"I don't care. I'm not a prostitute!" I said once again.

"Okay, dear," Emily said, moving closer to me. "You'll need to read and sign this. Then we can let you into Singapore."

The document they handed me was titled Registered Sexual Deviant."What?" I said, laying down the document. "I'm not a sexual deviant or a prostitute."

"It's for you own protection, mister, or is it miss?" Paul asked.

"Really," I said with sarcasm.

"Why yes, if you're arrested for male prostitution."

"Again!" I stated.

Paul interrupted, "Or for any reason. I know you're not a male prostitute. The point is, you will not be put into the male or female population in our jails. That would not be civilized. You would be put in a safer and secure place for...ahh, you're kind."

"Okay." I sighed and started to read the short one-page document.

"And," Emily leaned over and said quietly, "it's safer for you, and it's the only way you're getting into Singapore."

I signed the document, declaring myself a sexual deviant.

Paul signed it, Emily witnessed it, and Paul gave it an official stamp. He returned my passport and left the room. Emily stood by with a small smile on her face. Emily seemed like a reasonable lady, so I decided to ask a reasonable question.

"May I change?" I said, gesturing to my pile of women's clothes.

Emily looked a little surprised. She considered it then said, "I can't leave the room." Seeing the disappointment on my face, she continued, "If you don't mind." As she turned a chair around facing the door, with her back to me. "I'll just sit here. Take your time."

I packed as I changed. When both myself and my luggage were all together, I said, "Thank you so very much. Thank you."

Emily stood and turned around. Smiling her approval, she opened the door to the main lobby. "Enjoy Singapore, my dear!" And I did!

A female benefit is having doors opened for you, chairs pulled out for you, and bellmen to carry your luggage.

The valet opened the cab door for me. The driver opened the trunk, and the bellman gathered up my luggage. As he passed by me, he offered to take my briefcase and showed me to the desk.

I had booked the room as Miss Lisa Wynn. I approached the desk clerk and announced myself "Reservations for Miss Lisa Wynn, please."

"Yes, miss," he said happily. "We have your reservations right here. You requested an upper-level room, possibly with a view?"

"If possible," I said

"Passport, please," he asked.

"Of course." As I dug through my purse, getting out my passport, driver's license and the sexual deviant paper I had just acquired. I presented them all at the same time. He quickly copied them for his records and hand them back to me. He printed out my registration and handed it to me for my signature.

Identity

"Miss Wynn. I have a very fine room for you, second floor from the top with a beautiful view across the city," he added as he handed me my key.

"Thank you," I said, taking the key, and noting the room number. "Pardon me, but can the bellman take my luggage to my room? I need a little time."

"But of course," he said with a slight French accent. I wondered where that came from. Gesturing to the bellman, he handed him a note with my room number on it.

"Please take Miss Wynn's luggage to her room," the desk clerk said to the bellman.

I tipped the bell man twenty Sing, that's ten dollars, American.

Then standing in the middle of the busy lobby, alone and not moving for several minutes, I must have looked a little lost.

"May I help you, miss," a distinctly British voice cooed near my ear.

"Where's the bar!" I stated. What was I thinking? That was a bit direct, and even worse, it could be taken as a bit male.

Turning to the voice, I was greeted by the sight of a tall elderly gentleman in a suit, no less, with a complete head of white hair and white mustache. There was no mistaking him; he was the prototypical British statesman.

I was not expecting that and was quite taken aback. I froze, but only for a moment.

Softening my voice, I quickly explained, "I have been flying for two days straight. I just got off the airplane, and I need a drink in a room that is not moving."

He smiled and, with a slight bow of the head, said, "I completely understand, my dear. May I join you?"

49

"Well, yes, okay" was about all I could muster.

"Right this way." As he presented his arm.

We walked a short distance to the lobby bar. It was quite spacious with a view of the street, a few tables on the patio, and a comfortable and elegant lounge. He selected two lounge chairs facing each other and gestured for me to have a seat.

I sat and crossed my legs, showing a little leg.

The waiter soon approached, asking if we would like a cocktail. I thought for a minute and ordered a gin martini with five drops of red vermouth. The gin part was in honor of my British gentleman, and the vermouth was because I like it that way.

"I'll have the same but without the vermouth," he ordered.

I sat back and wondered if he was hitting on me. And if so, what should I do?

A slight smile crossed my face.

We sat and chatted for some time. I learned his name was John Chambers, and he worked for an English bank. He was in Singapore to check the books but admitted later that he was only there to confront the banker when there were some problems, and Singapore banks had frequent problems.

John thought I was both charming and interesting. I went on to describe my conference in Singapore.

John invited me to dinner. "I don't know." I gave the obvious line.

Yes, yes you do, I screamed to myself. *You have been flying for days and deserved a decent dinner with this charming and flattering man. And I wanted to continue the conversation. Besides, I want to see what happened next.* After a few moments. "Well, okay. But please give me a little time to freshen up?"

"Very well," he said in his nice British accent. "Shall we say about seven in the lobby?"

"Very nice," I said, trying to put on a little English accent. John gave me a funny look. I won't try putting on an accent again.

I hurried upstairs to my room. "What a beautiful view," I said to myself, as I lingered at the window for only a second.

I quickly showered off two days of travel, freshened up my makeup, and slipped into something sexy that showed off my good points and hid all that bad stuff, I hoped.

John met me in the lobby, extended his arm, and escorted me out to a night on the town.

We had dinner at a crab house right on the bay. The restaurant was a two-story building with the wall facing the bay completely missing on both stories. It was a bit odd; however, the view of the ships in the harbor, with their anchor light competing with the stars and moon for my attention, was awe inspiring.

We dined on black pepper crab, the best ever. Smaller side dishes of fish, rice, and vegetables accompanied our meal. John picked out a wine that matched our meal perfectly.

Again, John offered his arm, as we exited. Always his arm! Was that just a British thing, or was it me? Back at the hotel bar, we continued our conversation. He seemed to be a bit older than I first thought but extremely bright.

Over our cocktails, he broached the subject that had been hanging in the air all night. And he did it in a polite and friendly way.

"Lisa, you are a lovely woman, smart, successful, a wonderful conservationist, and with a quick wit. All the things I love in a woman. But..."

Oh, here it comes.

51

"I have two very important things I must tell you. I do this only in hopes of continuing our newfound friendship."

What now? Has he found me out? Is he looking for a male prostitute? What?

"One, I'm married to a wonderful lady for forty-five years. The love of my life. And two, I am impotent."

What does this all mean? He's married and important?

"Just how important are you? Like an ambassador or something?" I asked. John looked at me for what seemed minutes. He smiled a little and looked down.

Looking up at me again he said. "Not important, silly girl. Impotent, I-M-P-O-T-E-N-T; I can't get it up."

"Ohhhhhh." I giggled. "I see. Oh, so sorry" I laughed. "I wasn't laughing at you." As I giggled again. "Oh, I'm so sorry."

"That is all right," he said with a straight face.

I couldn't quit giggling. "I'm sooo sorry. I can't stop giggling. Please forgive me."

"I forgive you, my dear."

"And you were about to get lucky!" I finally blurted out.

His face exploded with laughter, throwing his head back, slapping his leg, one more loud roar!

The patrons in the bar, the bartenders and the servers all turned to see what was so funny that it was worth upsetting the quite hushed decorum of the fancy bar at one in the morning.

John waved them off with a flick of his hand. Grinning at me, he lay back in his chair and said after a short pause, "It would have been my honor to have gotten luck with you. I think we shall be good friends. In fact, I was the one who is lucky to meet you," he followed up.

I melted in my seat. "And I you. May I call you Sir John?" It just seemed so right to me.

"An honor, Miss Lisa," he said.

"Well, my conference starts tomorrow. I hope to spend some time with you before I leave. How long are you going to be here?" I asked.

"Another fortnight, I'm sure," he answered.

"And just exactly what is a fortnight? I'm American, you know. I think in yards not meters," I said.

"A fortnight is two weeks. In yards." He smiled. "And you, how long are you going to be here?"

"'Til Monday. I wanted to take a few days after the conference to see Singapore," I said.

"May I join you? I know Singapore quite well."

"For sure." I wasn't sure if I should kiss him on the cheek or shake his hand. I just gave him a little wave and a curtsy.

Sir John had planned a complete weekend. A trip to the Singapore Zoo started after tea. It was a wonderful place to visit; the animals had, for the most part, very natural habitats. I had never seen a black-on-black leopard; they had one, all black with black spots. The black spots were of a different texture hair, so one could see them.

After a light lunch and cocktails in the zoo's outdoor restaurant, we waved down a cab. We next visited the orchard garden with every kind of orchard there was, from the size of a chickpea to the size of a soccer ball.

Finally, we went back at the hotel bar, and over our martinis, we decided on an extra special dinner. That called for a complete makeover, hair to toenails. Next door to the hotel was a nice salon with an opening in less than an hour. I hurried my shower and then spent the next hour being primped, polished, and waxed.

Hours later, I met Sir John. He had changed into all white, including socks, shoes, slacks, shirt, dinner jacket, and a blue ascot. It was so 1940s but so British, so dated, so absolutely charming, and so Sir John.

He was standing at the bar and insisted I sit next to him with my back to the bar. I crossed my legs to show as much leg as possible. I knew he wanted to show that an old bugger like himself can still attract beautiful, leggy women.

Standing there, sipping his martini, he surveyed the patrons at the bar, enjoying every glance in our direction and every little whisper behind view-blocking hands.

Soon, his elbow came out, and we slowly crossed the bar and lobby to the cab waiting just outside the lobby door. I swished my hips as much as possible. We chatted all the way.

Dinner was at the famous Raffles restaurant. The restaurant was a mixture of old and new world: high ceilings, crystal chandlers, mixed with Asian touches, fine linens, silver, and china. This was one of the hottest and trendiest restaurants in all of Asia. Some said reservations had to be made weeks or months in advance. The food was overseen by a famous French chef. The food was definitely French with an Asian flare.

After dinner, over our cocktails, Sir John asked if I had ever been to the White Elephant. "You haven't? Well, we must." Sir John explained that it was the oldest bar in Singapore and, though not as plush as Raffles, was perfectly inhabitable.

The White Elephant sat by itself, surrounded by ancient trees and gardens. The structure was modeled after a southern pre Civil War plantation mansion. The White Elephant was all lit up that night; the white paint and columns was a sight to be seen.

Identity

The location was near the center of downtown, on Orchard Road, near the park that the customs agent, Paul, had told me about.

By the time we arrived, it was near eleven o'clock, well past the time that the police had cleared the nearby park of hookers and sexual deviants.

The interior was old, worn, elegant, and so British. Sitting at the bar, Sir John insisted we have Bombay martinis to complete the British image. The image in Sir John's mind was of a handsome British gentleman on the town with his sexy American girlfriend, completing a wonderful and elegant day.

As I sat chatting with Sir John on my right, a Chinese gentleman in a business suit approached me from the left.

Without hesitation or manners and very tipsily, he said, "I give you five hundred to have sex with me tonight."

The clunking sound was my jaw hitting the bar. I was stunned into silence. The blank expression on my face caused him to explain his bid.

"Five hundred American." He said as he counted out the hundred dollar bills onto the bar.

With my mouth still open, I leaned back in my chair and looked at Sir John.

Sir John leaned forward and just looked at the man with no expression on his face.

As I looked back at the Chinaman, I saw the blood drain from his face. He absolutely went white. He was so pale, I thought he would pass out.

"Mr. Chambers so sorry. So sorry. I did not mean anything, I apologize. So sorry. And to your lady, I also apologize. So sorry."

He literally bowed his way out of the building, leaving his five hundred American dollars on the bar. No amount of coaxing or offering could get him to come back to get his five hundred American dollars.

I turned to look in amazement at Sir John. "He's the president of the bank I am examining," he explained.

We both exploded in laughter. It was all I could do to keep from spraying the bar with gin. Every time we took a sip, we had to cover our mouths, as we exploded again and again in laughter.

After a few minutes, I looked at the money on the bar. "What should we do with it?" I questioned. "Can you take it back to him tomorrow?"

"It's yours, my dear." As Sir John gestured to the bills on the bar.

"What? I can't take it. That would make me a whore. Please take it back to him."

"What? And embarrass him some more? Believe me, my dear, the last thing he wants is his money back." Sir John was right. "Besides, he would just deny that he was here at all tonight."

We sat in silence for a few moments. I then called the bartender over.

"What do you think it would cost to buy everyone in here a drink or two tonight?"

"I don't know, miss. Why do you ask?"

"I was just wondering. Can you make a guess?"

"Oh maybe six or seven hundred Sing," he said.

I pushed the five-hundred-dollar bills toward the bartender. "Then buy everyone in here a drink, and keep the change."

The bartender had overheard and observed what had just happened, as had almost everyone else in the White Elephant. The bartender broke into a very big grin. "Very generous, miss. May I ask your name?"

"Miss Lisa," Sir John spoke up.

"Ladies and gentlemen," the bartender announced. "Miss Lisa, here." He said as he gestured toward me. "Is buying you all a drink and providing me with a big tip."

The bar broke into cheers.

"Three cheers for Miss Lisa." Someone with a heavy English accent shouted out.

"Hip hip hooray! Hip hip hooray! Hip hip hooray!"

Oh, how British, I thought, as I stood and curtsied to the crowd. As Sir John and I left the White Elephant, someone called out, "Enjoy Singapore."

"Oh…I am," I said.

Chapter 7

Leaving Singapore, I felt more confident with my Registered Sexual Deviant papers. It turned out I had zero problems leaving Singapore. Emily was checking passports; she had recognized me in line. Taking my passport and stamping it, she said, "Miss Wynn, I hope you enjoyed Singapore."

"Thank you, Emily. Thank you for helping me." A short pause as I collected my passport. "And I did."

***

It was closing in on 3:00 p.m. when Lisa pulled up in front of her business. The cabbie helped bring in her things. After opening the door Lisa pointed to a spot just inside the door. "Right there is good." Then she handed the cabbie his fare plus a ten-dollar tip.

Paula, seeing her first, rushed over and hugged her. "Welcome home. Why didn't you call me?"

"International flight. I never know when customs will finish having their way with me." Waving a hand in the air and then fishing through the pile on the floor for her briefcase.

Heading for her office, Anna squealed and rushed to give Lisa a big, consuming hug. They all headed into Lisa's office.

"How was it?" Paula asked.

"Great. No orders but lots of introductions to top people here in the US. It seems I'm going to be quite busy over this next year. I mean top companies like Apple!" Lisa paused.

"Cool," Paula said.

"Did you meet anyone?" Anna went straight to what was important to her.

"Why, since you asked, I met a British gentleman. I call him Sir John," I answered.

"Wow. How romantic. Tell me more," Anna said.

"It was romantic and platonic," I said as Anna looked puzzled. "He is about seventy, married, and important. I mean impotent." I chuckled.

"Important how?" Anna followed up.

"Not important, impotent. Dear, he can't get it up," I explained.

"Well, did you try?" Anna asked.

Lisa looking up for guidance "He's seventy and married!"

"So..."

"Anna, good God no."

"Well..." Anna opened her mouth to say something then, thinking better of it, closed her mouth.

I opened my briefcase and began taking out papers.

"Wait," Paula said. "You must be exhausted. We'll take an early dinner and then take you home. I'll call it done!"

"Sure. Give me an hour then we'll leave." I kept pulling out papers from my briefcase and started sorting them on my desk. They kept sitting there 'til I gave them the "what" look.

Paula said, "Yes, ma'am. An hour."

***

Exactly an hour later, Anna stuck her head in my door. "Asian food?"

60

"Hell no," I answered "Steaks?" She followed up.

"No." Thinking for a second and before Anna could guess again. "Italian." It was the only cuisine I could think of that I had not eaten in a while, and it's a comfort food. My stomach was looking for some comfort.

Anna turned and called to Paula, "Italian."

"Ah, Lola & Giuseppe's Trattoria." Paula called back. "Now drag her out from behind that desk. Dave's here. Her luggage is loaded up, and we'll meet you there."

***

At the table, we relaxed and ordered a bottle of wine before the menus could even be passed around.

I pulled out a piece of paper from my purse. "And I thought TSA was tough." I passed around my Registered Sexual Deviant document.

"What the fuck?" Were the first words out of Paula's mouth.

"Yep, I'm registered now. But we all knew I was a sexual deviant all along." We all laughed.

"TSA makes me prove it. Singapore makes me register." I continued, "Tomorrow, I'm getting my new passport."

I told them some of my Singapore stories over dinner. By six thirty, I was fading. Dave and Paula drove me home, and Dave carried in my bags, as I kicked my heels into the corner. I kissed them goodbye and struggled upstairs to my room. I showered away thirty-some hours of airline stink and quite literally fell naked onto the bed. I grabbed the edge of the coverlet, rolled over, and fell into a dream-filled sleep.

***

The next few months, I made the most of my Singapore contacts. Some weeks, I would conduct business in three states and five cities then fly home to spend the next week in the office.

On one of my extended trips, I was invited to spend a long weekend at Dr. Lora's beach house. Dr. Lora was there with her boyfriend, Dr. Jim. The visit gave me an opportunity to discuss medical options with the two doctors and collect some references.

Sitting on the deck one late afternoon, Dr. Lora leaned over and felt my breasts. "They seemed to have come out well."

"You used him first. Yours look great."

"I'll show you mine if you show me yours?" Dr. Lora said.

We stripped to the waist and studied each other's breasts for scars and firmness. Dr. Jim also took the opportunity to closely examine our breasts also for scars and firmness. A little too much firmness studying.

The three of us sat there, sipping wine and watching the last of the day slip away, topless.

After that relaxing weekend, I was back on the road, airport to airport. I had rented so many rental cars, I nearly forgot what kind of car I owned.

Houston became a pivot point for me. I would spend the weekend in Houston, and then I could pivot to any place in the south-central states in just a matter of hours.

The Weston Oak Galleria became my Houston home. Living in an upscale shopping center had its benefits.

The Galleria had street-level and lower-level parking. The Weston Oaks had unique elevator access from the lower lever that allowed you to avoid the lobby. You simply put your key card in the slot. On the punch pad, I would put in my floor. If it matched your key card, one of the four elevator doors would open taking you directly to your floor.

I thought it was cool. It later became essential.

If I was in Houston on a Saturday, it was Baba Yega time. Baba Yega was a relaxing and unpretentious even with a beautiful koi pond in the open patio. The bartenders were fun, the food was good, and the bar patrons friendly.

I usually wandered in around late afternoon, just after the late lunch crowd thinned out.

On one Saturday, I had enjoyed a ceviche for lunch and was on my second glass of wine.

I was sitting quietly, scanning through a copy of the Houston Pulse and stealing a glance here and there of a man sitting three seats away. He was kind of attractive in a rough sort of way. He was enjoying his fish tacos and a beer. He had been more obvious, looking over at me.

Eventually, he said, "I've seen you here before, haven't I?"

"Maybe. I'm in here every month or so when I'm in town," I said.

"So you're not a local?"

"No. I live in Chicago," I answered.

"And you're?" He asked.

"Lisa from Chicago," I answered, not giving to much information.

As the conversation progressed, he made his way across the two seats to sit next to me.

"Betty" he called to our bartender "Lisa's glass is empty. This one's on me," he volunteered.

He was good. He kept the focus on me. He was flattering and inquisitive.

"Betty, please," he would say, touching my glass more than once. "So you're here on Saturdays. What do you do on Sundays?"

"Sundays, you can find me at the Houston Museum of Fine Arts. I think it's one of the top ten in the world," I continued on in our conversation.

"Really," he said. "I do a bit of collecting myself. Mostly local artists or at auctions." As he leaned in.

"So what's your most interesting piece?" I asked. The conversation drifted around with a bit of give and take; he seemed to be judging my taste in art.

He made his move. "I got some pictures at an auction last year. They told me they are Erte's gouaches. In fact, I got two. Both are costume designs. I don't know if they're prints or not."

"Of course, if they are real, then they are original. Erte never made prints of his gouaches."

"Well, I don't know?" He said, setting out the bait.

"I've only seen one Erte gouache, and that was at an auction about five years ago. It sold for nineteen thousand dollars, and that was cheap," I said excitedly.

"Want to see them? You can tell me if they are real or not. I only live a couple miles from here. I can drive you over and bring you right back." He said setting the hook.

"No, I don't think so." But my curiosity was getting the better of my judgment.

After a few just a minute. "Well, okay. Just to see them. I'll follow you." I wasn't going to be at his mercy to bring me back. Besides, it was getting late. It was about nine at that point.

Identity

I parked in front of his condo. The street was wide and not well lit. There was a small yard, and each condo had a single walkway up to the front door. He parked in his parking space in the back. He came through the back door and opened the front door, welcoming me in.

As soon as I stepped in, he grabbed me and pulled me to him, forcing his tongue down my throat. When he let me go, I backed off and turned away to compose myself.

Suddenly, my head exploded as he smashed it into the wall. I was stunned. He grabbed me again and threw me face down on the floor. My head and chest were on his carpet, the rest of me on the brick floor of the entry way.

As my senses began to come back to me, I felt my arms being pulled behind my back and my hands held together by what later turned out to be a silk tie.

Holding my hands tightly, he used his other hand to pull up my skirt. He began tugging on my panties. I don't know if he was trying to rip them off or pull me up on to my knees. At any rate, he succeeded at both.

Then he raped me. I tried to scream, but nothing came out. I was coughing out blood. I don't know if it lasted thirty seconds or thirty minutes. I felt him expand then ejaculate; a few seconds later, he pulled out.

He let my hands go as he stood up and pulled up his pants. He headed around the corner down the hall.

"That was nice" was all he said.

As soon as he was gone, I jumped up. There was blood on his carpet, torn panties thrown by the door. I grabbed my purse and rushed out the front door, running to my car. I stopped at the car door and fished my keys out of my purse. It seemed to take forever to find them. As I stood there, I could feel the blood running down my legs and face.

I finally got into the car, locking the door before starting the car and taking off.

I stopped at the first stop sign and leaned forward into the steering wheel. No one was behind me. God, I need to call the cops, was my first thought. I caught my breath and held it. I had been hyperventilating. I took out my cell phone, holding it in my hands. I studied its face. I hesitated. Great, I could see the headlines, *Male Cross-Dresser Claims Rape*. Yep, some sick people will find that funny. Worse yet, I could imagine how the authorities would treat me. My track record with the authorities had not been good.

Car lights came up behind me. All I could think of was that it was him coming after me. I took off fast.

I parked on the lower level near the elevator. The parking lot was nearly empty; it was around ten o'clock. I sat in my car, taking inventory for the first time. I had a cut above my left eye and a bloody nose. That must have been the blood I was spitting up. The tops of both feet were bleeding as were both of my knees. I had a cut on my right calf, and I was sitting in blood.

Looking around to make sure I was alone, I quickly made my way to the elevator, my key card in hand. I pushed in my key card and punched in my floor. The elevator went directly to my floor. Now I had to make it down the hall to my room. I peeked out of the elevator, and I thanked God no one was around.

Safely in my room, the door locked and barred. I quickly stripped. I again checked myself out, this time with a clearer mind. Most of the bleeding had stopped. I stepped into the shower with the water as cold as I could stand it and for as long as I could stand it. When I stepped out I used the hotel provided mouth wash. I figured that was as close to a disinfectant as I could find. I used their cotton balls to dab at my wounds. I put a bandage over my eye and several, in a line, on my knees. My butt had quit bleeding, but I balled up some toilet paper and stuffed them in my panties just to be sure.

With my nightgown now on, I curled up in the fetal position. I had taken three Lunesta sleeping pills. I should have been knocked out with that many pills, but it wasn't 'til four that I fell asleep.

Sunday afternoon, I had a private conversation with one of the Baba Yega owners. Before I said anything, I was assured of privacy. I was told that he would never again be allowed in Baba Yega.

On Monday, I flew to Kansas on business. I didn't go home 'til Saturday. Paula called that afternoon "Hey, we're at Arrow. Where are you?"

"Paula, I'm not feeling well. I'm going to take a nap. See you Monday."

"What the hell?" I heard her say as she hung up.

I didn't nap. I called my doctor and saw him that afternoon. I had some damage but not serious. He didn't think there was any STDs; however, the results would not be in 'til Tuesday.

That weekend, I spent going over what I did wrong. What did I do? Yes, I was a little drunk but not that much. I didn't eat much all weekend.

On Monday, I put on a lot of makeup then dark hose and, finally, dark sunglasses. I was hoping to disguise my beat-up face and legs. Paula knew there was a problem right off.

She followed me into my office and closed the door. Studying me for a minute, she said, "What happened?"

"What? Nothing." As I arranged papers.

"You can't fool me. You got a black eye and a cut over your eye, and I'm guessing you're wearing dark hose for a reason." Coming around the desk, she took my face in both hands. "Now what happened?"

I slowly fell apart, sobbing; she took me in her arms. "What happened, sweetie?"

"I was raped" was all I could say.

It took quite a while for me to calm down. When I did, she gave me back my dark glasses. Paula called out to Anna to clear our schedules.

"What? Why?" Anna asked

"Because she's tired. I need to take her home. Just do it, okay. I need you to watch the place. Okay?"

We walked out, and she took me home. We talked all afternoon. Paula cooked dinner and sat up with me 'til I fell asleep. She spent the night in her old room.

The next morning, over coffee, I said, "Thank you," and took her hand.

"I've been there, remember that." As she pointed to a small scar over her left eye.

"Okay," I said, straightening up, looking around. "Okay. It's time for me to move on. That bastard has taken enough of my life. Now, I've got to live it."

"Way to go, girl." Putting her hand up for a high five.

***

On Thursday, I was back on the road. A month later, I learned that Sonia had died.

Identity

I went to Pittsburg to take care of business and to see that Sonia's ashes were laid next to her husband's.

By Friday, I had finished up all the loose ends, including all remaining business issues. That completed my last ties to Pittsburg.

I headed to the Pittsburg airport.

Chapter 8

I was leaving Pittsburg; I had been there all week on business. I was dragging my carry-on down the air bridge then I stopped and, for thirty seconds, took in a poster touting *Fabulous Hawaii*. I turned on my heel and left the air bridge.

At the closest counter, I booked the next flight to Hawaii and left thirty-five minutes later. In San Francisco, during my layover, I made reservations for a room at the Marriott by the beach in Hawaii. I shut off the cell phone; with its black face staring at me, I closed the red cover and slipped it into my purse.

Some sixteen hours after I walked off the air bridge in Pittsburg and booking a flight to "Fabulous Hawaii," I was walking into the evening sun in Hawaii, still wearing my business suit. I had been wearing business clothing for a week, month, year, years. I didn't remember. In the cab on the way to the Marriott, I opened the window and, breath after breath, drank in the balmy air until I hyperventilated and became dizzy.

At that moment, I was lost to the world. No one knew where I was; no one could get a hold of me or a hold on me. I was free of meetings, the phone, conferences, paperwork, questions, silly questions, relationships. I listed a dozens of people—oh God, mostly the people that I was free of.

By the time I got to the Marriott, it had grown dark and was getting onto the evening side of night. In the hotel, I found I didn't have much in the way of casual clothes in my carry on, mostly business clothes and shoes. I did have exercise shorts and a T-shirt that read, *Stop the World—I Want to Get Off*, an Anthony Newley play. I had forgot to bring tennis shoes for working out. It was just another symptom of my drained mental condition. I put on my exercise shorts and the T-shirt and sat on the balcony, taking in the evening ocean, the sound of the small waves on the beach, the sight of lovers walking hand in hand as they talked in low intimate voices, interspersed with loud boisterous laughter. What could possibly be that funny?

The Marriott had provided two pair of flip-flops in each room. They were expecting or planning for couples. Not this time, it was just me. I hate flip-flops, but it's all I had.

Flip, flop, flip, flop. I walked across the lobby, stopping only to ask the porter for quick directions and then walked on to the street. Several blocks down the street was a line of tourist shops. I bought a long T-shirt that had named my left breast *Hawaii*, a short khaki skirt, and a pair of cheap wedges. Out of impulse, I bought a notebook with a rough map of the islands and the word *Hawaii* on the cover, and finally, a big straw bag decorated with palm trees and the word *Hawaii* to carry all my newly purchased clothing items.

Walking back toward the hotel, I stepped into a liquor store. I shopped up four good bottles of wine. I mean, like over $25-a-bottle good wine! The corkscrew I purchased went into the big bag.

A little further on, I stopped in front of a Hawaiian-looking restaurant. It was quiet, mostly because most of the diners had already filed out. Still, enough people were left to warrant just one more patron.

I seated myself off to one side, arranging my purchases on the floor against the wall. Water and a menu soon appeared. Shortly thereafter, a glass of wine appeared. While waiting for my dinner of fresh native fish, I had about fifteen minutes to myself. Humm. Not much to see, nothing much to do. My sensible self asked my current self, *What the hell are you doing?*

The answer given by the waiter was "Be careful the plate is hot," a sensible and direct answer, not without a subtle meaning.

The Marriott porter, remembering my *Stop the World—I Want to Get Off* T-shirt from hours earlier, saw me struggling with my purchases. I, now was carrying my big straw bag, both wine bags, and my purse which had slipped down my arm was nearly dragging on the floor. He rushed to help. He carefully placed my bags on the bell cart. By then, the lobby was emptying and the restaurant on the ground floor was empty except for two die hards drinking at the bar. I noticed the table settings. What really caught my eye were the wine glasses. "Excuse me. Do you think they would mind if I took one of those wine glasses up to my room?" After a quick look around, I scurried in and snagged the nearest wine glass, not giving the porter time to answer.

Once more alone in my room, I looked out toward the darken ocean and starry sky beyond my balcony. Knowing how uncomfortable the chairs placed on the balcony were, they had just the plastic straps slung from one side of the frame to the other. I opted for the comfortable overstuffed chair just inside. I pushed, lifted, pulled, and in short time, wrestled it out on to the balcony.

With wine glass in hand and going on my thirty-first straight hour, I contemplated the sorry state of my life and what caused me to step out of it. How, in spite of all I have accomplished and everything I had accumulated. Why was I so unhappy? Just what was the secret of happiness anyway?

I started going over my divorce both of them, being jilted, then jilting, the kids, work, getting old, lost youth and other losses.

A few hours later, I found myself walking along the beach, wine glass and wine bottle in hand. Walking along the water's edge, with little waves sometimes chasing me up the sand, licking my toes and sometimes even higher.

I felt betrayed by marriage, by my kids, my lovers, by work; even time had left me. It seemed that the world had abandoned me. Not that I had abandoned the world.

I had tried, goddamn it. I could not make the world happy. I wasn't happy.

I sat in the sand, empty wine glass and empty wine bottle beside me. I was going over each and every put-down, insolvable problem, loss, and love loss. My self-esteem was at its lowest ebb.

Then, through the prism of wine and exhaustion, I clearly saw myself. *Well, myself, glad to meet me,* I almost said out loud. So what do you have to say for yourself?" I did say that out loud. "What's the secret to happiness?" That's a question, not an answer, I said to myself.

The sun sent feelers into the sky then kissing the tops of the oceans waves and crashing into my eyes. I realized that people could make me smile and often cry. But they could not make me happy!

I leaned back in the sand, letting the sun jump from the waves, warming my face.

I could no longer hold on to those sad, lonely thoughts. I let the lies and betrayals leave me. I lifted them up, and they just slipped from my hands, across the sand and into deepest depths of the dark ocean. Exhausted and now empty, I now realized, that no one and nothing could make me happy no matter where I was or who I was with, because only I could make me happy. My happiness or sadness was all up to me.

A peace settled into the empty spaces. A twinge of happiness began to build in my chest.

I blew a kiss to the sun and started back toward my hotel. A smile slowly took over my face. I knew the secret!

Chapter 9

The bright sunlight came streaming through the window, crashing into my eyelids, burning my eyeballs.

"Oh, what time is it?" I said out loud, as I pulled a pillow over my face, shutting out the sunlight.

Where the hell am I? Was the first thought that came into my foggy brain.

"Another hotel, I guess? Doesn't feel like home." As the days before came slowly, ever so, drunken night slowly to me, and now the pass few days without any sleep, came into view.

Oh, I think I'm in Hawaii! I almost said out loud. "And I know the secret!" I did say that out loud. As the night before hit me as bright as the morning sun light. *Morning? What time is it?* Four seventeen, the bedside digital clock announced. *Got to be p.m.,* I thought, as I threw the pillow on the floor.

I inspected myself. Naked and smelly but no worse for the wear, I thought. "I've been far worse," I said aloud.

As my feet hit the floor, I stretched and yawned and quickly put my arms down. What a smell.

I followed the trail of clothing back toward the bathroom. Panties, then bra, followed by T-shirt and shorts and just inside the door flip-flops. I hate flip-flops.

I quickly used the toilet then took a deep breath. I faced myself in the mirror.

"I take that back. I have never been worse," I said aloud to myself. Scratching my head, I found sand in my hair then in other places. Bloodshot eyes, wrinkles I have never seen before, and mascara running down my face like Alice Cooper had done my makeup. "Oh, God, help me," I called to any deity who was within earshot.

I brushed my teeth to get rid of layers of God knows what. Then I brushed them again and brushed my tongue, the roof of my mouth, the inside of my cheeks, and my teeth again. I spat out blood.

The room had the luxury of a shower and an oversized tub. I started hot water in both. The blessing of a good hotel is lots of hot water. I showered, washed my hair, and scrubbed the first layer of skin off my body. Then I lay down in the hot tub. I tried to soak it in, but my attention span, at two minutes, had reached its max, so I shaved the woolly parts of my body clean and my legs also.

I dried and fluffed my hair with the hotel dryer. I stepped back, threw back my shoulders, the throwing was more like wiggling, sucked in my tummy, and I took the Playboy pose. *Not bad, girl.* I thought, considering what I had to start with.

I followed the trail of clothing back into the bedroom, picking up and putting on the T-shirt and panties.

I noticed the small coffeepot on the desk and quickly made myself a pot of black gold!

The chair I had wrestled on to the balcony was still there.

Then it came to me that the maid had not knocked on the door to see if I was in and to make up the room. I glanced at the door, and the *Do Not Disturb* sign was not there. Then it had to be on the outside of the door. My God, it worked!

My cell phone was on the desk. I picked it up. *Still off* I thought, again I thought *still off.* Then I said it this time out loud. "Still off."

76

Maybe I should turn it on? Maybe just to see if Paula was looking for me? Not likely, I thought. Its black face was just looking at me, hypnotizing me, saying, "You want me baby, don't you?" For seconds, maybe minutes, I stared at that blank face.

The coffee was done. I poured a cup, looking at the cell phone. I thought you're just like a leash, pulling me back, keeping me in check. "Don't wander off too far or for too long," it was saying. "I'm your master. Mind me, missy."

"Not today, babe," I whispered to the phone. "Not today, babe." Slipping into the chair on the balcony, I sipped my coffee. *What a beautiful day*, I thought. *When have I noticed that it was just a beautiful day?* The sky was perfect with just enough clouds to give it perspective. The ocean was incredibly alive. Even the sound of kids playing in the pool and parents calling after them to be careful made the perfect moment I needed just then.

I thought I had learned the secret. I let my sober mind play with that thought.

Kids, exes, friends, lovers, cops, firemen, waiters, strangers, none of them can make me happy. Even Paula and Anna can't make me happy. I myself can only make me happy. Maybe I should figure this out in the most basic and shortest phrase possible.

With some effort, I worked my way out of the chair, poured the last cup of coffee, and retrieved the notepad from my straw bag and a pin from the bedside table.

Settling into the chair again, I said aloud again and again, "Let's see."

The Secret, I titled the page. *Only I can make me happy*, I wrote on the notepad. Looking at it, it didn't seem quite right. I scratched out the word *only*. It still didn't seem right.

This secret is harder to write down than I though. It seemed so easy. Okay, let's began again. *I am...* What next? *Can make...* No, not right. Okay, again. *What am I? How do I become happy?*

Again. *I am...? I can make me happy.* Not right. Works but it's not the secret.

I am responsible for my own happiness. Okay, looks right. The secret is to take responsibility for your own happiness.

Don't let other dictate, demand, require you to be happy.

Okay. That's the secret, and I'm sticking to it. And I'm starving. "I'm responsible for my own hunger," I said. "I'm responsible for finding food," I said louder. *This is fun.* "I'm responsible for my own happiness," I shouted off the balcony.

Chapter 10

It wasn't long before the lights along the shore began to glow in the fading evening light. Then as the numbers grew, they began to take over the last vestiges of the fading sunset.

The bear in my stomach began to demand more attention. I need food, I thought, and a drink. I had packed for success. I had only business suits and a high-impact CEO dress in my suitcase. I also had the few things I had bought the night before. I wasn't too clear-headed when I bought them. They had limited places I could wear them. Diving into the shopping bag, I found a khaki skirt and wedges. I had not thought to buy a blouse. *What a dunce. I can't wear the Hawaii T-shirts over a khaki skirt.*

I'm not wearing that Anthony Newley T-shirt. I thought, Maybe a white blouse. I had two of them with the sleeves rolled up and the top button, maybe two undone, they might be acceptable in public. The wedges finished off the outfit. *God, I've got to get a different purse,* holding up my practical, fashionable, and business-like Purse. "Oh well," I said, as I stuffed the notebook into it. "Okay, lady. Let's meet the world or what's left of it."

The porter met me in the lobby as I was wandering around. "Aloha, miss. How is your evening?" He asked with a smile.

"It just started, but it won't be long night tonight," I added. "I'm in need of a little comfort food. Is there anything close by?" I questioned.

"Well, we have a fine restaurant," he said as he gestured toward the right.

"I'm not dressed fine," I joked. "How is your bar food? Any chicken wings?" I asked.

"But of course. This way please," he said as he led me toward the lobby bar.

I took a barstool as far away from people as possible. I ordered a martini and my chicken wings. Not looking up, I took out my notebook and studied *The Secret. If I'm responsible for my own happiness, what is the opposite of that?* I flipped the page.

I'm responsible for my own sadness. Well, that is not part of this process. It's more like, I'm not responsible for your happiness or sadness. Okay, but that is not completely true either. What if I'm happy and everyone around me is not happy? Doesn't my happiness tend to make other people happy? Doesn't it rub off? At least a little bit? Well, that didn't write down so well.

Am I responsible for other people's happiness, I wrote. *Of course not.* I drew lines through the thought. *Am I responsible for other people's sadness? I have a couple of exes who would agree with that. No. I'm not even going there.* I crossed that out with vigor.

Okay, again. *What am I responsible for with others?* I paused. *What are they responsible for…for me?* Oh, man, this is getting messy.

My martini was near empty, and my wings had just arrived. There is no ladylike way to eat wings. You just got to pick them up with both hands and dive into them, getting sauce around your mouth and chin, and if you are not careful, on your cheeks and forehead also, just like I did, brushing hair out of my face. Not to mention wing sauce, free falling only to be caught by the balcony that my breasts and white shirt provided.

Another martini appeared. The bartender gestured across the bar to the blonde, saying, "Compliments."

Oh God, I'm not in the mood for this tonight. I glanced up to see a blonde lifting a glass. Smiling, the blonde seemed to be trying to ignore an intense conversation between a marine and a cute blonde girl standing nearby.

"Thanks," I murmured. "But please tell whoever that I'm busy and don't want to be disturbed tonight. Sorry," I said.

"The martini is still yours," the bartender said and turned away.

"Okay, thanks. Sorry," I said, mostly to myself, looking down at my notebook. *It's messy*, I thought. *By rejecting whoever sent me the martini, am I making whoever feel bad? Is it my responsibility? I didn't ask, flirt, wink, or any of the other subtle and not-so-subtle things a woman can do. And anyway, I'm such a mess and kind of gross with wing sauce all over my face and on my white blouse. So what is my responsibility?* I thought. *I don't know*, I admitted.

Everyone has to take responsibility for their own happiness, and if I don't cooperate, it's still their responsibility. *Oh shit! This is messy. I'm going to my room. Then I don't have to deal with this, whatever this is.*

I quickly down the second martini, and with a half-smile and a wave to the blonde, I made a beeline for the door.

***

Damn. They moved my chair back inside. Well, that won't do. Again, I pushed, shoved, and dragged the chair out onto the balcony. Then I neatly replaced it in the room with the strappy, challenged chair. Later, I would add a note to the maid that read, *I like it here. Keep my overstuffed friend on the balcony.*

I opened one of my back-up bottles of wine and poured a bit into my purloined wine glass. I settled into my comfy chair and flipped open my notebook. At the top, I had written *The Secret is I'm responsible for my own happiness.*

Now the messy part. What else am I responsible for? To who— whom am I responsible? For that matter, who is responsible for what to me? Why didn't whom work in that last part? Is it who, or whom? Don't get off track, girl, think.

I put my name on the first page. Then on each additional half page, I added the names of people I thought I might have some responsibility to, or for, or something. *Whatever.* I put down my kids' names. *That was easy.* Then Paula, my best friend and part owner in my business. Anna, who was more little sister than my blood little sister. *Exes? No, I wrote them off long ago. No, I better add them. Other friends or family...no, that gets too messy.*

Slowly, I tried to fill in the pages. I found myself crossing out a lot of what I thought other people were responsible to me for. Then I started crossing out things I felt I was responsible to other people for. I had an empty half page facing me with no name. I wonder who, whom, I'm missing? *Maybe it's who?* Oh well; the bottle is empty and the martinis have taken their toll.

I undressed and looked around for my nightgown. It was missing in action. I must have left it on the back of the hotel room's bathroom door in Pittsburg. Well, back to the T-shirt and panties.

What am I missing? Well, tomorrow I'll work on it.

I fell asleep, thinking. *Who was that blonde? What in the world attracted whoever to drab and messy me? Did they just feel sorry for me? Or did they just like chicken wing sauce all over my face? God, how messy could I be? Check that. I was worse last night or was that this morning?*

ALOHA! NO PROBLEM, MISS

Chapter 11

This morning, well, almost noon, was quite different from yesterday. I felt rested and a little bit happy with myself. I wasn't the cuss ball I was yesterday. The shower felt invigorating, and I felt like joining the world again.

I dressed with what I had, khaki skirt, wedges, and a white shirt with, oh yes, chicken wing sauce on the front. First things first, I've got to go shopping!

Down in the lobby, my friendly porter greeted me. "Aloha, Miss. It's a fine day isn't it?"

"Aloha, why yes it is. I'm looking for...by the way what's your name?"

"Porter, Miss." Pointing to his name badge.

"I know, but what's your real name?"

Again pointing to his name badge. "Porter, miss."

"What does your mother call you? What does she call you when you have done something wrong?" That usually got a longer response.

"Porter Allen, quit doing that right now!" Was his response.

"You're not kidding me. It really is Porter. How neat," I said. "My name is Lisa, so glad to meet you, Porter."

"Pleased to meet you too, Miss Lisa."

"Well, Porter, I need to do some cloths shopping obviously,"

I said, pointing to the stain on my blouse. "Where is a Macy's or Neiman Marcus or even a Target."

"Miss Lisa, you'll find Nordstrom and a Macy's in the shopping mall. It's a bit of a distance. I'll call you a taxi."

Nordstrom had a coffee shop just inside the door. I needed a cappuccino and a little something to eat. Pointing at my blouse, I told the attendant, "I don't need a napkin. I've got my blouse."

The next several hours were taken up trying on clothes and shoes. I came away with four comfortable but sexy outfits, one sexy scarlet cocktail dress, five pairs of shoes, a new purse, a sexy silk nightie, and a new suitcase to carry everything in, and my last selection was a wide-brimmed straw hat with a scarlet band to wear in the sun. I left Nordstrom wearing a short blue skirt, red tank top with a blue Hawaiian shirt over the tank top, open, but tied at the waist, strappy red platform wedges, and all topped off with my new hat.

I literally bounced into the lobby. I had chosen to go bra less. Not a very good idea at my age and boob size, but I wanted to feel the freedom, and I haven't gone bra less in public...ever; I felt liberated. Besides, the tank top had a little shelf built in to subdue the bouncing.

After dropping off my purchases and changing purses, I felt like taking on the world, or at least living in it.

"Hi, Porter. Can you point me——"

"Aloha, Miss Lisa," Porter said.

Oh, I get it. "Aloha, Porter," I said and he smiled. "Can you point me in the direction of some shops and restaurants?"

"Sure, Miss Lisa. Not more than two blocks from here, up that way." Porter pointed.

I soon came across a nice restaurant. Bagatelle was a 1900s two-story captain's home with a long wraparound veranda. The young lady at the receptionist's stand was wearing a traditional strapless Hawaiian dress with a white orchid in her dark hair.

"Aloha." I opened with that greeting. I could get used to this.

"Aloha. Table for two?" She asked.

"No, just one. I'm not expecting anyone else, alone, all by myself, just the three of us; me, myself, and I." I smiled and noted that I was being very talkative, not at all like last night or, for that matter, the last few days, or was it years? "Could I get one of those tables along the rail?" I continued like I hadn't said all that stupid stuff.

As she ushered me toward my table, she said, "Oh. You're such a pretty lady. I'm sure you won't be alone for long," as she glanced at my untethered breasts.

Sure, I thought. *Like these girls are going to attract a lover.* Settling down I placed, my hat on the chair next to me and took my notebook out of my purse.

Looking at the title page, *I read, I am responsible for my own happiness.* Well, I guess I knew that deep down, all along. How else would I explain why I was here in Hawaii? I left because I was unhappy, but with what? Exactly what?

Why did I catch that flight to Hawaii? To get away from everyone and everything. Why? *To find myself*, I wrote in the notebook. It suddenly became clear. I had lost myself. I had lost myself to work, kids, exes, my sometimes family, even the few friends I had left. I was so worried about doing a good job; making my kids happy; keeping exes, if not happy, at least not unhappy with me. As far as the family went, I was just trying to keep them off my back. I was trying so hard to make everything good and happy that I lost myself.

Okay, now I can go back to the separate sections for each person. Half pages weren't doing it, I made each their own page.

The waitress came by my table. "Aloha, will you be having lunch with us?"

I looked up for the first time. "Ah, water; excuse me, Aloha. I'm a bit new here. I'm forgetting my manners."

"No problem, Miss." She said as she gave me the Hawaiian signal for "no problem" the index and little finger pointing out, and at waist level swiveling her hand back and forth. I noted the gesture and promised myself to use it on Porter.

"Thank you, and, I don't know. Maybe a mimosa, I guess; thank you."

It was then I noticed I had a clear view of the beach and the ocean beyond. *Oh, that is breathtaking*, I thought. The reason I was here didn't matter much right then. My eyes were flooded with the view, my lungs feasted on the clean ocean air. I was lost in paradise, and time had no meaning.

"Have you decided on lunch, Miss?" The waitress asked as she set down my mimosa, a beautiful drink in a tall glass. The recipe is just champagne and orange juice with an orange slice on the rim.

"No, I'm sorry, I haven't even looked at it yet. The view is incredible."

"No problem, Miss," she said giving me the sign again. "Take all the time you need. Just signal me when you decide, or need another mimosa. Enjoy the view."

"I tell you what. When you see my glass a quarter full, just bring me another. I might be awhile, if that is okay?"

She gave me the signal, smiled, and said, "Take all the time you want. It's a beautiful day. Enjoy it."

I gave her the signal. "Thank you." See, I'm learning Hawaiian. My gaze returned to the view. My mind cleared itself. I had no special thoughts, just the pure joy of feeling good, nothing else. Just good and happy. I sat pen in hand; notebook in front of me for I don't know how long. Long enough to cleanse the soul.

Eventually, I put down my pen and sipped my mimosa. I put my head in my hand and just enjoyed the view. My mind and body drifting out over the sand and ocean, headed nowhere; just being.

"You seem much more relaxed today!" The words brought me back, at the speed of light, into my chair along the railing, my head still in my hand. My mimosa was three quarters gone.

"What?" I asked, as I was snapped back to reality. Well, as real as reality could be just then. "What?" I asked again.

"Aloha. I said, you seem much more relaxed today."

I looked up to see, sitting just across the aisle for me, the blonde from the other night who had not sitting there when I came in. I did not see anyone come in. I had been lost in my own special world of light and happiness; the smile still on my face. "Why yes, yes, I am. You were at the bar last night," I said, still smiling.

"Yeah, you seemed so lost in thought last night. I'm the one who bought you the martini."

"Excuse me?" I commented, my expression changing. "Why?"

"You looked kind of depressed. I thought you could use a drink," the blonde answered.

My expression and body hardened at the thought of being stalked, cute blonde or not.

"Look, I'm not stalking you," the blonde said, figuring out

why I stopped talking and was staring. "We are staying at the same hotel. I was walking by here and saw you again. I thought I could use some lunch. And maybe say hello, and you looked much more relaxed. Maybe I should just shut up now. Are you waiting for someone? Damn, not my business. I really should shut up now, pardon me if I disturbed you; I should leave now." The blonde said, rising from the chair.

"Thank you for the martini," I said giving the sit down hand sign. The stuttering had won me over.

"You're welcome," the blonde said, a little relieved.

"No, I'm not here with anybody. Just me and myself." I stopped myself from going into the me-myself-and-I routine.

"Then, well, may I join you? I'll buy you another, what is that?"

"Mimosa."

"Mimosa."

Chapter 12

First, I met Miss Dana.

"Mimosa."

"Mimosa"

"I can buy my own mimosa thank you very much." I said with a little chill in my voice. I waited a few seconds, just long enough to see some disappointment in her eyes. "But please sit and join me." I said with a smile gesturing towards the chair across from me.

"The blond" stood up. Her blond hair just below the ears, she had blue eyes and was tall and athletic. *WOW*, my mind said, *WOW!* Her black tank top showed her high, firm if smallish breasts. Her nipples were clearly visible, if not distracting. I looked down to check mine, yep visible. Her white Levi mini skirt highlighted her hips and long smooth legs.

"I'm Dana." She said as she sat down. "So happy to meet you." She was clearly comfortable with her sexuality.

"I'm Lisa." I said a bit jealous of her awesomeness.

"Tell me Dana..." I asked her, as I leaned forward, showing a little cleavage of my larger size C plus breasts. "Really, why did you buy me that martini. Do you have a thing for messy women with wing sauce all over their face and blouse?"

"Ha ha, no. Well yes, you so easily handled the mess, you were interesting. And, as I said, you looked like you needed a martini. You were sitting their scowling over your notebook, kind of lost in thought. I like people who think" Indeed, Dana did not know any women who would dare be so messy in public and still act like it didn't matter.

My mimosa was near the bottom of the glass. The waitress showed up, on cue, with another mimosa. Dana gestured toward my drink and said "Aloha. Can I have one of those mimosas? They look very good."

The waitress said yes. And as she turned away from Dana, she looked down at me and smiled as if she knew something I didn't.

"Besides" Dana continued "I saw you earlier, and you looked like you just worked out some deep issues."

"Earlier? When? Where?" I was a bit puzzled.

"Yesterday, at about dawn. In the lobby you were very cute. All sandy and a little disheveled. Carrying an empty wine bottle and wine glass."

"Oh God." I hid my eyes.

"No. You looked great. Like you just solved the problems of the world. Do you have a thing for dawn, wine and sand? "

"You do have a thing for messy women, don't you?" I said looking up.

Dana quietly smiled. She was a good judge of women, who was a possible partner and who wasn't. Lisa was clearly a possible. But, there was something else, something she could not quite put her finger on.

"Yes." I said assertively "Yes. I have a thing for all three. Yes, I was sandy, drunk, and just watch the sun come up. But, I was on a mission."

"And what was that mission? It must have been very important? Was it a secret mission?" She asked, smiling.

"How did you know it was a secret mission?" I let the question hang in the air. "The mission was to find myself, and I succeeded. I found myself sitting on a beach in Hawaii. I walked up to myself, and we had a long talk. And finally, around dawn myself told me the secret." That was about as precise as I could put it.

"Interesting. What's the secret?"

"Well, the secret is..." I leaded forward and whispered. "I am responsible for my own happiness."

She sat and thought a bit. "Are you sure? No one else can make you happy?"

"That's not the point. It is my responsibility to be happy. To accept happiness, or reject it." I so wanted to take out my notebook right then and write that down.

"OK. A philosophy, I can dig it!" She said.

"It's really not that simple. I'm working through all the messy parts. That's why I was unresponsive last night, no offence; I didn't want to be disturbed last night. I didn't need to be disturbed"

"And today?" She said.

"And today I can buy my own mimosas. Thank you very much." I said with a smile and a little giggle.

"I would like to hear more about the messy parts." She smiled back with her own little giggle.

"Maybe someday." I backed off. "I think now I need to order some food." As I picked up my menu.

"Sounds good." As she picked up her own menu. "What do you fancy?" She asked with a smile.

"Aloha." She called to the waitress. "We would like to order two more mimosas and Lisa, what would you like to eat?"

We sat and chatted. Dana was trying to understand this woman, Lisa. Dana knew most men were attracted to her and intimated by her. She flaunted her femininity but always with a touch of aloofness and always in control. But, this woman was different. Lisa was softer more feminine more open but in control, used to control. This was a mixture Dana had not known.

Quite a while later Lisa called for separate checks. It was well past five o'clock, it was several hours till sundown.

"Dana. It has been wonderful. But, now I need to enjoy some sand, ocean and a little late sun." I made ready and collected my things, rising ready to leave.

"That sounds awesome. Walking at the water's edge." She said trailing off. As I stood, she added. "I'm not doing anything right now."

"Would you care to join me?" I offered.

"I thought you would never ask." Dana said as she stood up. I'm five foot ten inches, tall for a woman, and with 3-inch wedges, I was all of six-foot one-inch tall. Dana stood, she was wearing flats, and was still taller than me. For a few seconds we stood eye to eye. Blue eyes to blue eyes, only inches apart. I froze for a hypnotic moment.

"Excuse me." I said breaking the trance. "I need to use the ladies room."

"Good idea" Dana said "especially before going out on the beach."

We both used the toilets and Dana neatly washed her hands, and just glanced in the mirror. I, on the other hand, lingered behind to brush out my hair and freshen up my make-up.

Upon returning to the receptionist stand. Dana was chatting up the cute receptionist, asking about the beach and the best and closest places to go. I interrupted to thank the receptionist. She smiled and looking down at her seating chart, avoiding eye contact, she just said "Enjoy the beach."

Dana led me out the door and onto the street. Reaching the sand, we sat on a bench and removed our shoes. I was wearing my new sun hat. I had my shoes and purse in hand. Dana had her shoes in hand and her small purse thrown over her shoulder and across her chest thus clearly delineating her breasts. We walked the water's edge.

With the water sometime just below our knees, we enjoyed the warm Hawaiian sun and cool pacific waters. We started to learn more about each other. First the obvious things, I lived in Chicago. Dana lived in Atlanta. She had a grown daughter, Alyssa, who lived in Atlanta. I had grown children, a daughter Bridget, in Los Angeles, and a son, Sean, in San Francisco.

I explained that I had married early, and divorced not early enough. Then married again soon after.

"You were married twice?" Dana exclaimed. "Once wasn't enough for you?"

"Well, you know love and all that stuff." I defended. "But the second time was much better. I was going through a lot of changes at that time. Jessie, my second, was so supportive. It just got to the point that I had to move on. It wasn't Jessie's fault. It was all me, all my fault."

"Well, once was enough for me. That man just didn't understand me." Dana filled in. "I mean he didn't hit me or anything like that. Besides, he knew that I could take the little bastard. The best part, it made my dad happy, I never knew my mom. And as a bonus, he got a granddaughter, before he passed. I'm happy for that anyway."

Dana went on to explain that she was an art dealer. Buying and selling art to studios, interior decorators, and more than a few collectors. She had only one employee, her daughter.

I had a company that made very small parts for other companies. I had too many employees.

Eventually, we sat in the sand and watched the sun go down. As the last rays of light danced their last dance of the day, across the tops of the darkening waves. As the sun slid towards tomorrow, Dana put her arm around my waist. She turned to me and said. "Hi Lisa" and lightly kissed my lips.

I let the kiss linger on my lips. Then turned my gaze out to sea. I needed a moment, to collect myself, and understand what just happened. Dana, sensing I needed a few minutes, turned her gaze seaward.

"Sorry," she said. "If I miss read the signals. I thought, well, that you liked women. That you liked me, are like me."

"I do like women. Always have. I do like you, but I'm not really like you." I tried to explain without giving away my secret.

"I see." She said disappointed

"I really liked the kiss. I haven't been kissed in a long time. A really long time, I was just a little surprised is all." I tried to explain, as I reached for her hand. She took it for a second, and gave my hand a squeeze.

We sat quietly for a few more minutes, taking it all in.

Shortly, she stood and offered her hand to help me up. I took it, and after standing, held on.

With the hotel lights showing us the way along the water's edge. The sky, newly illuminated by the first evening stars provided us with a romantic view. As we walked along the water's edge toward our hotel. We didn't speak much. We were each lost in our own thoughts. Each of us looking into space; looking at the stars, but also looking into ourselves. We both were thinking *What now?* From two distinct vantage points.

As we reached the hotel, Dana broke the silence. She had come to some sort of decision, and I had not. "I know a nice club just down the street. It's a little noisy, but it has good music."

"I really don't know. Let me think about it for a few minutes," I said as we reached the hotel.

The hotel provided a foot shower to wash the beach sand off our feet. Dana held the valve open while I rinsed my feet. After rinsing her own feet, she stepped right into her flats.

"It's a mixed club. About half lesbians, then couples and a few gay men. But, really nice people" She was putting on the full court press. "And it has live music, killer martini's and...and I really don't want to let you go right now. Besides the night is still young." She waited as casually as she could.

I sat on a nearby bench. Shoes in hand, looking up at the stars. Knowing it was digging into her psyche, I waited. *The only way to control this woman*, I thought, *is to be in control.*

"Still thinking about it?" Dana asked.

"No, just letting my feet dry." I said holding up my shoes. "New shoes; I didn't want to ruin them."

"So, you're going with me?" She laughed.

Looking down, I nodded my head *yes* and smiled.

As we walked toward the club. Dana took my hand. I felt safe and comfortable holding her hand.

When we reached the club, Club "D", we were greeted by a short stocky woman with a crew cut, Hawaiian shirt and knee length pants and flip-flops; damn, I hate flip-flops.

" Aloha Dana. Who's your cute friend." She asked.

"Candice meet Lisa. Isn't she fabulous?" Dana made the introductions.

"She certainly is." Candice said as she stepped aside, welcoming us in. Walking away, it was only then that I realized that Candice was collecting a five-dollar entertainment fee. A fee Dana and I were not required to pay.

Club "D" was dimly but adequately lit. The group at one end of the bar consisted of a large woman singer who had a powerful voice, and who hit every note perfectly. A female guitar player who also did back up. A female base player who had a trumpet, and clarinet at her disposal. The piano player was a thin black guy with a Ray Charles voice.

The room was about three-quarters full, but the night was still young. As we made our way to the bar various women call out "Hey Dana." "Hi sweetie." "Aloha Dana." Clearly, Dana had been here more than once. I could understand how unforgettable she would be. After all, at about six-foot-two she was a full head taller than most women in the club. Her blond hair, blue eyes were not easily forgotten. She was after all a very beautiful woman.

We found seats at the bar.

"Club "D" is known for their martini's." Dana said as she gestured to the back of the bar. In a space behind the bar about four feet wide and going from ceiling to floor, shelf after shelf, filled with every band and flavor of Vodka one could imagine. To one side was a large list of about twelve martinis. I only recognized two, Cosmopolitan and Chocolate Martini's

"You have to order a martini tonight. I know you can pay for your own, but not tonight." Dana said.

"I only recognize the Cosmo and Chocolate martini's. I don't know what to order?" I started the list.

"Well I suggest that you start with a Marilyn Monroe." Dana said.

"Start!" I gasped.

"Well, you might want to try a Rainbow or a Tropical. I'd stay away from the Purple Crack. But Sex-On-The-Beach is always fun. Save it for last. It's the tastiest." Dana teased.

"Don't start, you." I said as I lightly slapped her arm.

"Two Marilyn Monroe's please." Dana ordered.

"Hi Dana." We heard someone call from behind. As she turned around Dana received a kiss full on the lips.

She could only be described as young and sexy. She was wearing a bikini top and shorts, with sandals. Somebody must have sent out a memo, because about half of the women there got it. Her hair went half way down her back and still had enough left over to brush across the top of her bikini, finding comfort in her amble bosoms.

"Oh, hi Fran. Nice seeing you again. I call her Fran because she's from San Francisco." Dana explained. "Fran meet Lisa. Fran, I forgot your given name? What is it?"

"I'm going with Fran from now on, way better than Mable." She said turning her back to me. "Later honey if you got time." She said quietly, but loud enough for me to hear. Turning to me she squeezed my thigh at an inappropriate height. "Nice to meet you, see you around." Turning, she quickly disappeared.

As our martini's arrived, I noted aloud "Cute girl."

"Yes, she's quite the package." Dana said, as she watched her walk away.

The music started up again, and that made talking difficult, so we just enjoyed our martinis.

Just as Dana was ordering two tropical martinis, another young, equally sexy woman, who had also gotten the memo, tapped Dana on the shoulder.

"Hi Sweetie" She said as she put both arms around Danas' neck and standing on her tip toes, gave Dana a quick kiss on the cheek.

"Hi yourself Lucy." Dana said as she untangled herself from Lucy's tentacles. "This is Lisa, she's with me. I'm showing her around."

"Oh" said Lucy as she backed off. "Well, see ya," she said as she melted into the ever thickening crowd.

I looked Dana full on, as she glanced away as much as she could. "What?"

"How was she?" I asked.

"What?" Dana tried to ignore what just happened.

"When you slept with her. How was she?" I asked straight out.

"I didn't sleep with her!" Dana defended herself.

"Really?" I knew the signs, I had seen them many times before, I was given a crash course in *Signs of infidelity 101* during my first marriage. You can't put this one over on me.

Blushing and looking away, Dana said quietly "Sleep was not involved."

"Hummm." I turned to the bar. A few seconds later. "That's OK." As I drained the last of my second martini. "She is one hot package, that one."

"Yes, and as I found out that night in the bar. The night I bought you a martini, married." Then pointing to a table next to the wall across the bar, to a guy who was obviously a marine or sailor. He looked vaguely familiar. "Poor bastard has his hands full."

"What would you recommend now?" I said touching the empty cocktail glass in front of me.

"Try a Mello Melon. I'm sorry if I disappointed you."

Identity

"No, no." I stammered thinking back to my notebook. I'm responsible for my own happiness. "No, I really didn't meet you 'til this afternoon. It's not like I'm your mama, or wife. No explanation necessary." *What made me say; wife? God I'm messy.* I was starting to feel the martini's.

"OK, if you're sure" Dana said turning back to the bar to order our drinks. Silence.

"Look, I told you a little while ago that I have not been kissed in a very long time, a very, *very* long time."

"Well." Dana started

"Shhh." I shushed her putting my finger to my lips.

"I liked it, the kiss, and just because, well because I haven't been kissed in years doesn't mean that you can't go around kissing anyone you like. Besides you only bought me five martinis. And..." I rambled on.

"What? I only bought you three martinis?" Dana said holding up three fingers.

"These three, the one you bought me the other night and the one more you're going to buy me." I giggled.

Setting down my half-full glass, my nails hit the stem knocking over the glass. I mopped up the bar with all the available napkins.

"See, messy girl." I said.

Dana was feeling her martinis as well. Started to giggle. And for the next few minutes could not stop herself.

"It's OK Dana. No big deal. Oh listen it's *Hallelujah* by Leonard Cohen, I just love that song." Looking down at my empty glass. "Sex-On-The-Beach please."

"What?" Dana said a little confused.

"Sex-On-The-Beach. You said it should be the last drink tonight, and believe me, it's got to be my last drink tonight." I was beginning to slow down my speech. A sure sign getting close to the edge.

We sat and listen to the music, sometimes we could talk, sometimes we couldn't and sometimes the music was too good to talk over.

As I was nearing the bottom of my sex-on-the-beach martini, Dana took a credit card out of her purse and called for the check.

I soon was gathering up my hat with a little Mello Melon on the rim. "I think I'll call you Mello Melon." I said as I named the hat in honor of the night.

"Good night." I said as I spun off the bar stool. All that moving was too much for my soggy brain. I did the two step, and reached out for the bar stool to gain my balance. Instead I was caught by Dana's hand on my upper arm. Holding me up right.

"Let's walk home, I mean back to the hotel. If you don't mind, I'm feeling a little tipsy. Can I hold on to you to steady myself?" Dana said.

I would think later, because I wasn't thinking too well at the time. What a smooth line. Someone not as smooth and nice as Dana would have said. "Call you a cab." Or the slightly better, "You're a little drunk. I'll hold you up and walk you home." But, no, Dana took it all on herself.

Dana put her arm around my waist, and I put mine around hers. Candace said good night, flagging us on out of the bar.

The fresh ocean air and the walking had a sobering effect. We enjoyed the stars. I even pointed out the satellites moving faster than the starts, just miles over our heads. Upon seeing a flaming meteor cross the sky, Dana wondered if it was a rock or space junk.

By the time we reached the Lobby, I was much more in control. I turned to say good night.

"I'll walk you safely to your room." Dana said, as I began to decline "You never know what kind of people might be staying here." She warned.

"You're staying here!" I noted.

"Exactly!" She smiled.

I laughed a little "OK, just to my door, not through my door. Outside my door, got it?"

" Yes my lady, got it."

My mind was still a little foggy. But, I kept thinking "No way, I'm not doing it, she doesn't know me, doesn't know about me. I'm not filling in the blanks, no ma'am. Not tonight."

When we reached the door, I took the key card out of my purse, and holding it tightly in my hand, put my hand behind my back.

"I had a wonderful time. I enjoy your company very much. Your an interesting and charming lady." I said "But, this is as far as you go." Holding my hat and purse in one hand and the key card tightly behind my back.

"I fully understand. No problem. But, may I have a good night kiss?"

"I thought you would never ask." I stepped a little closer.

She put both hands on my waist and pulled me close to her body. She then gave me a long, slow, wet, passionate kiss and pulled me tight to her body. My mind went blank. I dropped my purse and hat. She had sucked the air out of my lungs, leaving me standing. Still looking up. Dana politely picked up my hat and purse. Handing them to me with a smile, and a little bow she said. "Good night. May I see you tomorrow?"

"Aah, sure," was all I could manage, and gave her a little good bye wave.

She turned and headed for the elevators. I watch her go and admired what I saw for about a half a minute. The once white mini skirt, now had sand, bar stool stains and a little Mello Melon on it. But the dirty white skirt still showed off her hips. I'm sure she exaggerated her walk just for my pleasure. Sighing, I open my door.

WOW, my mind said, then my mouth followed silently, *WOW*, then the words came out. "WOW!"

What the hell am I getting myself into, I wondered as I prepared for bed. *I'm not ready for this, whatever this is? I'm just finding myself. Never mind. I will probably never see her again. Just like all the other women who have popped in and out of my life.*

Even if she wanted me. A big if. It wouldn't last. Long distance, you know. She might even be disgusted by me, as I have been told. "I'm disgusted by you." I can still hear the words.

So, I thought, followed by a long sigh. *I took responsibility for my own happiness today. And I was happy. It was my decision. All else is behind me.*

DRIVER, NEW DIRECTION

Chapter 13

It was 7:30 a.m. I was adapting to the time change. It only took thirty-six hours without sleep plus two more days. But I was getting close to my normal wake up time.

I was feeling a touch of leftover sex on the beach. I lay quiet with the pillow over my head for a little while. I started thinking about Dana. *Boy, that was some kiss. Maybe I'm just out of practice. No, that was some kiss.* Then remembering her walking away in that dirty white Levi mini skirt. *Nice butt.*

Okay, girl, out of bed; it's a new day. I threw the pillow across the bed.

I used the toilet, made coffee, grabbed my notebook, and finally got comfortable in my overstuffed chair on the balcony.

Looking over, I noticed the strappy chair I placed in the room still had the note on it. I guess the note worked. Or the maid knew that the crazy bitch was just going to rearrange the furniture anyway. I opened my Notebook. Okay, what was that thought I had yesterday? How did the conversation go? I am responsible for my own happiness. Here's the point. I can accept it or reject it! The question was can anyone else make you happy? I am responsible, so I can accept it or reject it.

So, can the people on my list accept or reject? "Chilling thought," I said aloud.

What did I learn from last night? Well, for sure, I am responsible for my own happiness. All those other sickening cute, young, young and cute, sexy

103

women, no, girls. They weren't old enough to be women. Who may or may not have been in Dana's bed are not my responsibility.

What am I thinking? Dana did make a move on me. Okay, from an earlier and soberer conversation, I can accept or reject. I've got to write that down. Oh yeah, the question was Can anyone else make you happy? My answer was to accept or reject. I wrote the question down and put several question marks after it.

But Dana put a move on me. Simple. Accept or reject. I'll apply that to me. I decided and started writing down the most difficult things that I have accepted or rejected or should have accepted or rejected.

I wrote on my own page. *Can I accept being called disgusting?* I did accept it. And I've carried it with me ever since. How do I get over that? I can paper it over with some of the nice things people have said of me, and I wrote some of them down, but the words, *You're disgusting,* still bled through.

The messy part is I didn't know at the time I could and should have rejected that. So now it bleeds through makeup, clothing, success, failure, pain and pleasure. I may have to go back to that person some day and say, "No, I reject that. I am not disgusting!" I wrote that down.

So, why don't I feel "disgusting" around Dana? I wrote that down. I went back to each person on my list and wrote down the worst thing I have said to them and the nicest thing I have said to them and then tried to think how that has colored our relationship.

I was lost in thought for over two and a half hours. It was after ten, and still there was no call from Dana. I felt my spirit sinking.

No, I reject that. Her problems are not mine. Well, I guess it might have been a messy date anyway. Date? What was I thinking? Dana made no suggestion that she was going to ask me on a date! *Dear, pitiful me, stand strong. I reject that thought.*

104

Identity

I need to get out of this room, I thought, as I headed off to the bathroom. I had taken off my T-shirt and panties and had just turned on the shower when the phone rang. I shut off the shower and picked up the phone on the bathroom wall.

"Yes."

***

Dana was having her own awakening well before she could fall asleep. She slipped into bed naked. Thinking first about all those cute, young, stupid things that came up to her tonight. Then she felt guilt. Why did she feel guilty? She never felt guilty before. Did she feel guilty about having sex with them? She never did before. So why now? *God. I feel like I never grew up, permanently caught in my twenties. Why in the world did I admit to Lisa to having sex with Lucy? My practice is to deny, deny, deny. It's a lot easier that way. Why Lisa?* She wondered as she fell asleep.

The next morning, Dana dragged herself out bed at 4:30 a.m.

That was a great kiss, was her first thought that morning.

She made her calls to Atlanta and then Boston, did her exercises, showered and dressed. Dana got her coffee and sat on her balcony. Her balcony was three floors above Lisa; neither one knew that little fact.

Her thoughts were about Lisa. *What is it about her? I can't put my finger on it, but she sure is interesting. Well, there is only one thing to do.* Dana called the front desk then dialed Lisa's room.

"Hi, this is Dana. Are you up?"

"Sure. I have been for a while," Lisa said.

"I've reserved a couple of lounge chairs on the beach. I've ordered mimosas for eleven thirty. Would you like to join me?

"Well, I'd love to but the sun doesn't like me. It always burns me up. I don't understand. I love the sun. So, no; I can't." Lisa backed off.

Dana's mind was searching for an answer. "Umbrella" came out of her mouth. "I'll get you an umbrella and sunblock, and wear a shirt, and I'll get a beach towel for your legs and..."

***

In my room, three floors below, I interrupted Dana. "Wait, wait! Stop already. You had me at umbrella. I'll take care of the rest," I said; happy at her desperate attempt to get me to the beach.

I had to calm myself. My brain was going through a natural high. *These emotional swings are making me dizzy.*

"Once more," I said. Then as casually as I could. "What time was that again?" Like I didn't know.

"Eleven thirty."

"Okay, I've got a few things I need to do. So I'll aim for eleven thirty. What time is it now?"

"It's ten twenty now."

"I might be a little late, so..."

"No problem," Dana said, adding, "I'll see ya when you get there. Aloha."

"Bye." I hung up.

Looking in the mirror, I thought, *Oh sure, that's easy for you to say. No problem. I've only got an hour and ten minutes to make myself look beautiful.*

***

In the lobby, I saw my friend, Porter. "Aloha. How is your day?" I said.

106

"Aloha," he said as he turned toward me. "Oh, just another day in paradise, talking to a beautiful woman."

"Okay, who is that?" I asked, looking around.

"Why, you Miss Lisa," Porter said, chuckling.

"Porter, I need sunglasses, sunblock, and a bathing suit, and a big beach towel and quick. Can you help me?"

"In the hotel shop to your right. A little pricey. I'll admit, but convenient, or..."

"No, convenient and quick is what I need. Thank you." I turned and took a few steps and turned around in mid step, foot still in the air. Looking back, I asked, "Am I supposed to say aloha when I leave?"

"Always appropriate," Porter agreed.

"Aloha." I smiled and waved. My Hawaiian was getting better..

I made my entrance, seemingly unhurried, and only about ten minutes late. Again, I made some improvisations. *I'm getting pretty good at this,* I thought. The swimsuit I selected was just that a full red swimsuit, not a two-piece or bikini. Over the top was my famous white blouse, minis, the wing sauce stain. My Mellow Melon sun hat and the sunglasses were a nice touch.

Dana was lying in her lounge chair in the sun. She was wearing a skimpy white bikini, bracelet, and sunglasses. God, she looked almost naked. I looked like a mummy, all wrapped up in linens and just out of the pyramid for a day in the sun.

Her lounge chair was placed next to mine, except my lounge chair was covered by not one but two umbrellas.

"Hi." I tried to think of something cute to say, but nothing came to mind. Dana sat up and turned toward me.

"Aloha, Lisa," she said as she patted the shady lounge chair for me to sit.

Then she leaned over to give me a kiss. "You smell nice. What are you wearing?" Dana asked.

"Oh, just a fresh shower and a little Red Door," I answered. Sitting next to Dana was a small table covered by yet another, but smaller, umbrella. Dana poured some orange juice into a champagne flute and topped it off with champagne. She then offered me some fruit. We talked and enjoyed the view. About an hour later, her cell phone rang.

"Aloha, Alyssa. How you doing, sweetie?" Dana said into her cell phone. "Just sitting by the ocean with my new best friend, Lisa." She said as she winked at me.

Dana listened for a few seconds.

"Oh shit, I forgot! I know, I know. When? I know, where? I know. Text me the details. I know. Okay, sweetie. Love you." She put down her cell phone and turned to me. "I forgot all about this thing." How would you like to go to an art exhibition this evening with me?"

"An art exhibition?" I questioned.

"Yes. There is a new artist here in Hawaii, who has recently become very popular in Atlanta. I have a client who wants some pieces. It wasn't my original mission, but it came up a few days ago," Dana explained.

"So, you have to work, and you want me to tag along?" I questioned.

"No, no. It's not like that. It's fun. They serve wine and champagne. They have lots of really good appetizers. I know the dealer, and he goes all out for these things. Please."

"So, I wander around, looking at art, drinking wine, and eating pâtés while you are in a back room somewhere negotiating the price of a piece of art?"

"No, well, yes; but it only takes fifteen minutes or so," she said.

"Did I say that was a bad thing? Take your time." I put my hand under my chin in a seductive way, looking off into space. "Excuse me, beautiful, do you think this might be Hawaiian primitive? You aren't married, are you?" I added, as a little jab at Dana's little blonde chickie.

"Ten minutes, that is all the time you have to seduce someone else. After all, you already seduced me." Dana said with a smile.

Well, I didn't expect that either. I better change the subject. I then asked, "Is this hoity-toity?" Dana gave me a puzzled look.

"Hoity-toity. You know, dressed to the nines. Cocktail dresses?"

"I guess. I'm wearing a short black sheath dress and black stilettos." She stumbled. "I have to look in control."

"In control of?" I teased.

"The negotiations. Oh, I get it. Not you. That definitely wouldn't be possible," she said with a wink.

"Well, you're going to look fabulous, and formidable," I added, thinking that in a tight dress and stilettos, she would both be dynamite and over six foot seven.

"Formidable, yes. That's the idea. Keep them off balance. They just keep looking at my boobs as I squeeze a few more dollars out of them." She laughed.

"Hoity-toity it is then. What time?" I asked, thinking that at six foot seven or so in heels, what else are they going to look at beside her boobs?

"What are you going to wear?" She asked me.

"Don't worry. It won't be black. You'll see."

"Around six o'clock. I'll pick you up." Dana settled back in her chair. "I know where you live." She smiled.

"Okay. What time is it now?

"About twelve thirty." As she checked her cell phone for the time. I started putting a list together in my head. The longer I sat there, the longer the list got. I casually sipped my mimosa. I figured I had to leave in about thirty minutes, so it wouldn't seem that I was in a panic. But I was.

"There will be appetizers and cocktails," she added.

"Yes, you said that," I said

"I'll make reservations at a hoity-toity restaurant for afterward," she continued; it was her chance to regain control, or so she thought.

Thirty minutes later, I sipped the last of my mimosa. As I rose up, I said, "I've got a few things to attend to. So I'll see you at six. Aloha."

***

In the lobby, I looked for Porter. *Where are you?* I wondered as a bit of panic rose to my throat. Finally, I saw him standing by the street side door. "Porter. Aloha, Porter. Please help me." I quickly moved on before he could talk. "I need a manicure and a pedicure and quick! Where is a good place?" I was sure he knew everything.

"Aloha, Miss Lisa. I don't know." Seeing my crestfallen face, he continued. "But, give me a minute. My sister uses some place close to here. I have heard her say how great it is." He took out his cell phone and tapped out a text.

While we waited for an answer. I looked around nervously. Porter was trying to hold my attention with some small talk about the day, or something. I really wasn't paying all that much attention.

His cell phone signaled an incoming call and he answered. "Aloha, sis. Here is the situation," he began, going on to explain the nail situation. "Lisa... Lisa Wynn. Okay, cool. I'll let her know. Text me the address."

"Okay. All set," he said. "I'll get you a taxi. When you get there tell them that my sister, Keri sent you. That will get you in early," Porter explained.

"Wait! Carry Porter. Your sister is named Carry? Really Porter, your sister's name is Carry?" I asked as I tried to suppress a giggle.

"I know, I know. We've heard it for years. It's Keri, spelled K-E-R-I, Keri. It's a Hawaiian thing. I'll get you a taxi," he said with a little giggle to himself.

I gave him a hug, as I stepped into the taxi. "Thank you so much, Porter, Aloha."

***

With the driving time and the waiting time, it was only an hour before I was sitting in the pedicure chair. The warm water caressed my feet, and the massage chair gently rubbed my back. Sally did my nails. Randy fixed my hair, so it looked more fashionable, not a full hairstyle, just some quick brushing, curling, and spraying.

By four thirty, I was back at the hotel. By six, I was powered, painted, and dressed. Sitting back for a second, I started thinking, *How did the gods of Nordstrom know I was going to need this scarlet cocktail dress and matching shoes? They were perfect except, except why didn't I get a matching clutch?*

Neither of my two purses were right. Shit! I looked around. *My cell phone case is red!* Not matching scarlet but red. I took the cell phone out. It was still off. I stuffed in my driver's license, hotel key card, a credit card and a few dollars; no room for much else. I tried to squeeze in my red lipstick. No luck. Well, between the girls was the only place left available for lipstick storage.

At exactly six came a knock at the door. As I passed by the bedside clock, I noticed it read six zero zero. I answered the door and stepped out.

Shutting the door, Dana said, "Wow, breathtaking."

"Thank you." Taking a step back, I looked Dana up and down. "My God, incredible. You know that Robert Palmer video, "Addicted to Love"? You look just like those crazy beautiful girls playing guitar except you have blonde hair and, here." Taking out my red lipstick from my bra.

"Really!" Dana said, taking a step back.

"No, really. You want to look dominating? Try this on." Motioning her toward the mirror across from the elevators, I handed her the red lipstick.

Taking the lipstick from me, she questioned? "Sure you want to go out with a lipstick lesbian?

"Just put on the lipstick," I directed.

Dana turned toward the mirror and applied the waxy red paint that women have been applying to their lips since before Cleopatra. "Perfect!" I said, blowing her a kiss. "Could you put that in your clutch? Not much room in mine," I said as I held up my chic cell phone clutch.

In the elevator, I asked, "How did you time it so that you got to my door at exactly six o'clock?"

She blushed a little. "I waited in your hall for ten minutes."

"Silly. I was ready fifteen minutes ago," I lied.

Helping me out of the cab at the art gallery, Dana took my hand and gave it a little squeeze and walked me to the door.

As we entered the gallery, the room went silent. All eyes turned to the very tall, striking woman in a mini black dress with the bright red lipstick. Her tall, but not as tall, redheaded girlfriend in an equally mini scarlet dress just might have been noticed. Both of us were wearing very high heels.

The congressman was the first to speak up. "Dana dear, wonderful to see you again." He invited us down the steps into the gallery. The crowd took note and went back to their chatting and discussing the art on the walls.

"So who is this redhead?" The congressman asked, taking my hand.

"Carl, meet my friend Lisa."

As we walked the gallery, sipping champagne and tasting the hors d'oeuvre, Dana introduced me to various people. The governor was there, and Dana introduced us. Both the congressman and the governor were clients of Dana.

After about an hour Dana, left me in Carl's care and excused herself. She explained that she had to do some business with the dealer in, of course, the back room.

I didn't wander much from Carl's side. I didn't need to; everyone of import or self-impressed import came by to say hello to Carl and introduced them to me. A prominent attorney slipped me his card—that's what attorneys do—and gave me a stealth pat on the butt. That's also what attorneys do.

I was flattered and impressed. I had never been treated like one of the most beautiful women in the room. Never.

Dana returned in about fifteen minutes, all smiles. We made small talk with Carl and a few other minor celebrities for the next half hour. Dana then suggested that we leave for the hoity-toity restaurant where she had made reservation.

This is the part that I was now dreading. Dana clearly had a physical interest in me. And I was more than interested in her. But I was not as I appeared, and now I had to tell her. This is where people usually run screaming into the night. Not really. Well, only once, maybe twice.

In the taxi, I gathered myself up. I worked up all the courage I could muster. "Dana, I need, I mean really need to have a discussion with you about...about the real me."

Dana put her hand on my leg. "What's the problem, baby?" With real concern. "Was it about tonight? Did something happen?"

I put my hand on hers, and she could feel me tremble in real fear. "I'm sorry. Can we go to that park bench we were at the other day? The one on the beach?" I pleaded.

Dana simply sat a second, noticing that I was serious, and said, "Driver, change course," and gave him directions.

As we reached the bench, she said, "So, we're here."

"Dana, I really, really like you. You're beautiful, smart, capable, funny, charming; I could go on, and on. And I so respect you. But I have not been completely honest with you. And I really, really don't understand why you have taken an interest in me." I began.

"Well—" she started.

"Shush! " I quieted her

Dana looked directly into my eyes. She did not smile, just intense concentration.

"Dana, I'm a transsexual. I started out as a boy, now I'm a woman. These are not my breasts, just silicon bags under my skin. My lady parts, my vagina, the doctor's made it out of my penis. It works. I mean it's useful. I can have climaxes. The doctors operated on me more than once. In about two weeks, I've another surgery. This time in Phoenix. But I'm not a complete woman I'm sorry, I really am." I waited in silence, for her response, arms folded, head down. It seemed like years.

The light went on in Dana's eyes as she put all the little details together. Lisa was very feminine, in control and used to control. She made use of every feminine tool: make up, dress, mannerism, and depended on others to protect her, open doors for her, look out for her, a real prototype lady. Not many of those around nowadays. She nodded as things finally fell into place. "How long have you been a woman?" Dana asked.

"I'm sorry.

How long since the surgery?"

"Over two years ago," I whispered. "I had my implants done about five years ago. It was then I made the decision to finally change my life." My whole body was shaking. "But I've always felt like a woman," I said, looking up. "I kind of felt like I was just having corrective surgery."

Dana looked out to sea then up at the stars. This obviously wasn't what she was expecting. "I want to make sure I say this completely right" she began. "Sex is important, not just for satisfying the sensory glands but for a complete giving of one's self. The intimate knowledge of sharing. But that is not why I'm interested in *you*, taken by you really."

I broke in, "Dana, I can have sex. I do climax. I just have to be careful."

"Oh, that's great." She gave a strained smile. "As I was saying," Dana said, "I mean, I want to get to know you better. Something in you, in us, is drawing us closer together. So it doesn't matter. You're more than your body. You are more than a woman. You are unique and fascinating, and you're different from any other woman I have ever dated. And I do want to get to know you better."

"I don't know why you are interested in me," I started. "I think you have to let what I told you sink in." Again I waited, fearing the worse, rejection. *I reject you!* Or worse. *You're disgusting! Oh dear God.* My body was in full fear mode. My skin rippled from the trembling in my heart.

Her hands were on the bench when she leaned forward, her head down. "I don't know, I really don't know." She contemplated. "I'm being honest here, I'm just attracted to you. I think you are the most interesting woman I ever met. So I just want to see where it goes from here." And after a few seconds "Just that."

"Well, I'm interested also. I would like to see where it goes." I went on, "At least you didn't say, 'Screw it.' Or, as I've been told, 'You disgust me.'"

"I would never say that," she said as her head snapped in my direction. Then looking away, she fell silent. She was concentrating, her eyes focused at some misty thoughts far out to sea.

The silent minutes began piling up on one another. I was trying, in the dark, to study her face, to try and figure out what she was thinking. Finally, in an effort to at least move things along, I said, "I know you're thinking lots of things. Let it out. What do you want to know? I'll answer every question honestly. From now on out, only honesty. I tell you anything you want to know." I thought for a second then asked, "Have you ever been with a transsexual?"

"No, I haven't. I've met one or two. At least I think they were transsexual." She continued, "Why did you, are you? This is weird."

I started to fear the worst.

"No. No, not you. The question, the question is weird. Are you a lesbian?"

116

"I guess I am now," I answered "But I've always preferred women."

"Why, again, have you? Didn't you change to be with a man?"

"No. I changed because I always felt I was a woman. I did try men, both before and after the change. I didn't like it much, sex with men. In fact, I don't like most men much period." I continued. "You were married, had a kid, so you must have liked men at one time?"

Dana thought a second. "I've always been attracted to women, girls when I was girl. But I was trying to be 'normal'" she said putting up quotation marks with her fingers, "but it didn't work out. Not for long anyway. After Alyssa was born, we decided, he decided it wasn't working out. He hasn't been around for or dropped by to see Alyssa since she was maybe four." Dana paused, thinking for a second. "Why don't you like men?"

"That's easy. I know them too well." I began "I was one once remember? Besides, I don't like stubble. It leaves my face and nipples raw. I don't like all that body hair or the smell. And most of all, during sex when they're done, they're done, no matter if you are or not."

"Amen to that," Dana said.

"Anything else?" I asked

Dana shook her head no, not looking up.

I thought she had made a decision, and I assumed it went against me. After a minute or so I said, "Then let's go back. I'm tired, I'm sorry." I really wanted to run. I was feeling like I did something wrong and got caught.

"Okay, want to walk?" Dana asked.

We took off our shoes. Dana reached down to help me up, taking my hand. She didn't let go right away. We walked the beach in silence. Not in the water, just along the sand, each in our own thoughts. I was ready to bolt, to run, to avoid pain, to avoid being told again that I was disgusting.

We eventually reach the hotel, and Dana walked me to my room. Taking the key card from my chic cell phone clutch, I held it tightly in my hand and placed it behind my back, just like the night before.

Dana didn't say a thing. She just put her hands around my waist and pulled me close to her. She slowly leaned in and gave me one of those long, passionate kisses, and as she did, both hands slid to my butt cheeks, grasping them firmly, pulling me to her body. I could feel her breasts against me and her hips against mine. Her right hand moved up to my breast; she didn't squeeze, she caressed it gently. The kiss lasted forever and not long enough.

As Dana released me, she took a step back. She just kept looking into my eyes for an answer to her unasked question. I took a deep breath. *It's now or never*, I thought. I took my hand from behind my back. I held out my hand and offered her my key card.

"Would you like to open my door?"

WHAT NOW, MISS?

Chapter 14

I had not been naked, completely naked in front of anyone, including my doctors, since my last marriage, since my operation. Come to think of it, I had not had a lover in over a year that did not run on batteries or the big boy that plugged into the wall.

So after Dana brought me to several climaxes over several hours, I fell into a deep, peaceful sleep until 5:00 a.m. That's when Dana jumped out of bed, leapt into her dress, and grabbed her stilettos. I was wide awake, but feigned that I was a sleep. She leaned over and gave me a kiss on the forehead and whispered, "Later." Then she was out the door.

I sat up in bed, shaking my head. I wasn't happy. "A kiss on the forehead, for God's sake," I said out loud. I looked at the clock. Five-o-five for God's sake, and she races out the door. Throwing myself back down on the bed, I tensed every muscle in my body. Then kicking and pounding the bed, let out an "Auggggggaugg" and more than one "Shit!"

The thought that passed through my mind more than once was, *Was she running off to get away from me? Or was it because she had to get ready for another date? Was I just a one-night stand? Shit!*

I rolled out of bed and headed toward the bathroom. I stopped at the full length mirror, looking at myself naked and thought, *Shit! Who wouldn't run away from this?* Then I quickly showered, made coffee, and fished out my reliable T-shirt and fresh panties, and covered the offending parts of my body.

But, oh God, I really liked her. Shit, shit, shit!

Again standing in front of the mirror, I asked, "What did I do wrong this time?"

Pouring a cup of coffee, I automatically picked up my notebook and pen then made my way to my friendly overstuffed chair on the balcony. The sun would not come up for quite a while. Still, I turned the chair, so it would catch the first warming rays of the sun head on. *No duck and cover today*, I thought. *Bring it on. Burn my face. Where are you?* I sat in quiet contemplation for quite a while. Then the sun left the ocean for the red and orange sky. I looked up. "Oh, you again, but you are so lovely, the way you kiss my face and warm my soul. But then, just like every other woman or man for that matter, you'll burn me in the end. Do I disgust you?"

I took a sip of my coffee; it had grown cold. Thinking of the kiss on the forehead, I slipped out of my chair and headed to the microwave, "Shit," I said again. *Forty-five seconds in the microwave should do it*, I thought.

Shit, shit, shit! Am I over this shitting thing? I thought. *No, just one more good shit.* "Shit!" I said out loud.

Back in my chair again, I looked down at the notebook. I started a page for Dana. I looked down at the name *Dana* and started writing. *Dana is responsible... For what?"* I thought.

On the next line, I wrote, *Love.* Then scratched it out, and a few minutes late wrote, *Love,* again.

She can't be responsible for my falling for her. I'm responsible for that, I reasoned. I wrote that down. *I am responsible for my own feelings.* I flipped to my page and wrote that down. Then I thought, *It's her fault that she's so goddamn beautiful, sexy, smart, sensitive, and damn good in bed.*

God damn her for running out on me, I thought, feeling sorry for myself. I found unwanted tears running down my cheek. Hell, I was warned. I know the signs; I saw them all. Shit. All of them. *She's a player.* I wrote that down. Flipping to my page, I wrote down, *How many times have I been played? Have I been a player?* Thinking back, once maybe, and that was when I was a man. *Really?* I asked myself. I wrote down, *Debbie, when I was a man.* Then I wrote *Sorry.*

I looked back down at my page. Reading *I am responsible for my own happiness.* And *I can reject it, or accept it.* Okay, let's go with that.

I am responsible for loving someone. Let's keep it generic. *Someone.* That's good, generic. I love my kids; my sisters; and my friend, whom I love more than my sister. So when you hand out love, is it unconditional? That's a crock! Love has all kinds of conditions. The conditions just depend on who you're loving. If unconditional is a ten, then kids are a nine; family fall between nine and, well maybe, a five on a good day; exes are between zero and five maybe, zero by definition. New lovers have all kinds of conditions. So if they live up to my conditions. "No problem," I said, making the sign. And if they don't, I can accept it or reject it, or change my conditions, or not. Got it. Now just write it down.

I was in the fog of writing and trying to understand what I was writing when the phone gained my attention on about the fifth ring. Slipping out of my chair. I looked at the clock on the nightstand on my way to the phone. *How did it get to be after nine o'clock?* I wondered.

Sitting down on the unmade bed, I answered the phone on the bed stand. "Did I wake you?" Dana asked.

Not sure of where this was going, I said, a bit on the chilly side, "No, I've been up for quite a while."

"Good," Dana said, not reading the tone in my voice. "I've reserved a table, this time by the pool with a big umbrella, for you. I noticed yesterday you're not a daytime beach person. The reservation is for ten thirty, is that okay?"

"Second," I said as I turned my head and grabbed a tissue and blew my nose and took a few second to collect myself and make a decision, accept or reject.

"Lisa, is everything okay?" She asked, a little on the "what's happening" side to her voice.

"A second please." Then not to be so cold, I added, "I'm all tangled up here." Covering the mouthpiece with my hand, I put the phone in my lap. *Dear God, help me. What am I letting myself in for?* I would love to be just writing this down. Writing all the reasons I should not. Not again. But maybe I should write down all the reasons I should say yes. No time. *Well, make a decision, girl. I have heard from my head. Heart, what say you?*

I made my decision. "Of course, I would love to," I said, smiling into the phone with a little laugh. "I would really love to." Now that was a bit too much. I didn't need that second "I would really love to." I hung up, wondering *how the hell am I going to keep this emotional roller coaster on the tracks?* I keep getting flung from one side to the other, up then down. What a mess.

I cleaned myself up as best I could. I opted for the blue mini, red tank top, and Hawaiian shirt. That was just the way she saw me the other day at the restaurant.

***

I was in the lobby by ten-twenty. Seeing Porter, I called, "Aloha," and quickly moved toward him and gave him a big hug.

"Well. Aloha to you too," he said with a little surprised look on his face.

"Thank you, thank you and please." Showing my nails. "Thank your sister Keri also. She's a godsend. Aloha."

"Have a wonderful day, Lisa. Aloha," he called out as I moved to the patio.

Dana was wearing a strapless black bikini, a black shawl wrapped around her waist, and black wedges. She had seen me come on onto the patio and was standing by the table, waiting for me. *What an amazing, beautiful Amazon woman*, I thought. Forget what the head and heart say. *What say you, thighs? I thought so.*

As I came up to her, she put her arms around my neck. I put my arms around her waist. When we kissed, I swear one foot involuntarily rose up behind me, just like in the movies. Some of the guests, who were enjoying Dana's centerfold image, turned to each other and whispered. We didn't notice.

"Well, I like the way you say Aloha., I said smiling. She sat me down and poured me a mimosa, and then slid into her lounge chair in the sun. I could not wait to ask. "Why did you run out on me at 5:00 a.m. this morning?"

"I'm sorry if I woke you, I tried to be quite." She responded, not answering my question.

"Not the answer I was looking for," I said directly with a little pout.

"I was scheduling with Alyssa, and then a conference call with a dealer organization. It didn't last very long. It's part of my work, and it comes off at 5:30 a.m. Hawaiian time. That's 1:30 p.m. Atlanta time. Sometimes, it lasts a few hours and sometimes three or four hours. I never know," she explained as she quietly sipped her mimosa.

"Oh, work," I said, just then realizing it was Wednesday evening in Chicago. Work was not part of my notebook. Paula was, but work wasn't. Oh God, I was so worried about finding myself that I forgot all about work and my best friend Paula.

Dana looked over at me. "You're mighty quite."

"I was just thinking of work," I said.

"I promise, no big art gallery exhibits today," Dana said, thinking I was speaking of her work.

"No. No. I liked it, I had fun. I got to chat up a congressman. And..." I paused for effect. "As a bonus, I got the card of a prominent attorney," I teased. Maybe it was a good thing to get away from work, unscheduled. *Maybe. I do miss Paula*, I thought.

"We can have the whole day to ourselves if you like." Dana continued.

I smiled. "I'd love that!" Thinking to myself, *as long as we don't see those sexy young bitches.*

After a second I asked, "Honey, can I call you honey? If you don't like it, I won't."

"Yes. I like," Dana said.

"Honey." Now I had to stop and think about how I was going to say this. "Humm." I cleared my throat. "Honey..." *Now that's honey too many times*, I thought. "You're an art critic, so how would you critique last night?"

"Well, it was usual, just about what I would expect to find in Hawaii. Her technique is excellent, if not a bit common; all-in-all, a good artist."

I lightly, scratched her arm, with my new nails. "Silly, you know what I mean. How was I? You know how inexperienced I am. Not that I haven't had experiences, but nothing like you. Sorry, let's say... How much more worldly you... Sorry again. How do I say this? Help me please?"

"Experienced is a nice bland term." Dana reached for my hand. "You were an excellent date. The men at the gallery were literally drooling over you."

"Ha," I said. "Then they were wetting their pants over you."

"Please, and the women at Club D; the young girls were all jealous of you! Really!" Dana said.

"You'll say anything to flatter me, it's really not necessary. But, that's not what was I after. The sex part, did I put you off? Did I ask you to do things you didn't want to do?"

"Hell no!"

"Wait! Did I do things you didn't want me to do? Be serious now."

She waited a second, thinking. Then she reached over and took my hand. "It was a perfect night. You were more exciting in bed than any one, or two women could ever be."

"You want two women?" I asked half in jest.

"No, just you. You're exciting and adventuresome okay? Now, how was I?" She said, throwing it back in my face.

Blowing her a kiss, and wiggling my tongue, I said. "Dreamy." I think it's easier for me to ask the kinky questions. So I did.

"Now, that we have settled that. Can I ask you about a few kinky questions? Easy questions for now."

"Kinky, okay. Like how?" Dana asked.

"I like ropes and hand cuffs, you know a little light bondage, what about you?"

"To be honest. I've never tied anybody up. But there are those who have wanted to see me in hand cuffs." She laughed. "But I have never tried it."

"Want to?" I asked.

"Me or you?" She countered.

I continued, letting the question hang in the air. "No whips, or chains, or pinching, or hurting; maybe a little light spanking, me getting spanked, not you, just on the butt but not painful just playful. No pain."

"Pain out, spanking in." She smiled nervously.

By her reaction, I knew that this was a new playground for her. She was interested and had probably contemplated bondage with others before.

"And I like my vibrators," I added.

"Can I meet them?" She joked. "Oh, wait, I did last night. Wonderful fellows."

"Buzz, buzz," I said, sticking my tongue out of my mouth, making a little butterfly motion.

"Oh God. Please don't do that." Dana was fidgeting.

"Why?" I asked in a low voice.

"Because you make me so horny. I want to just jump over this table and rip your panties off."

I slipped my hands down my waist to the hem of my skirt, and wiggled a bit. When her attention was drawn away, I slipped my panties down around my ankles. The other patrons were starting to notice, but not openly, but with smiles. I stuck my tongue out again. "Buzz buzz."

"Oh God. Please don't do that." Dana was fidgeting.

"Why?" I asked in a low voice as I continued to buzz.

"I told you. You make me horny," she repeated.

I just smiled. I reached down between my legs and took the panties off my ankles. I held them between my thumb and middle finger over the table. I could hear muffled laughter in the background. I ignored it and gave Dana my full concentration.

"God," Dana said as she grabbed my panties. Looking around. "You're asking for it, you know."

"No, I'm begging for it." I panted as I leaned across the table. Dana slid out of her lounge chair and slipped on her wedges. Putting the ice bucket with the champagne under one arm, she reached down and pulled me to my feet. Putting her free arm around my waist, she walked me toward the lobby.

"You know you deserve to be spanked for this," Dana said as we walked off.

"Yes, ma'am," I said as demurely as possible.

"Do you have ropes?" She asked.

"No, but I have several scarves that will work," I teased.

Passing through the lobby, Porter smiled and discreetly turned away.

In the elevator, I took out my key card, handing it to Dana. I said, "You'll need this."

Chapter 15

What if Dana was a straight male? Let's see.

"Mimosa."

"Mimosa"

"I can buy my own mimosa, thank you very much." I said with a little chill. I waited a few seconds, just long enough to see some disappointment in his eyes. "But, please sit, join me." I said with a smile gesturing towards the chair across from me.

"The blond" stood up. His blond hair just above the ears, blue eyes, tall and athletic. *WOW*, my mind said. *WOW!* As he stood up, I quickly scanned him. He had on a deck shoes, wearing knee length khakis shorts and a Hawaiian shirt with only the bottom three buttons buttoned.

"I'm Dana." As he sat down, offering me his hand. "So happy to meet you."

"I'm Lisa." And with a little twinkle "Like wise."

"Tell me Dana." I said as I leaned forward, showing a little cleavage. "Really, why did you buy me that Martini? Do you have a thing for messy women with wing sauce all over their face and blouse?"

The night before Dana had been standing at the other end of the bar. He was trying to smooth over hurt feelings and hide a short liaison between himself and Lucy. Lucy was the sexy, young blond girl standing next to him at the bar arguing with her husband, a marine just back from deployment.

Lucy had made up a story about being a single young artist in Hawaii for inspiration. Dana had fallen for it. Not really, but he wanted to believe the story. *It could have been true.* He forgave himself. Then, the next morning the marine called from the base to have his wife pick him up. She knew he was due back from Korea that morning? *Whoops...not again,* Dana thought. Dana had made another mess for himself.

Walking back to his room early that morning he saw this intriguing woman walking through the lobby, wearing a T-shirt, barefoot, carrying an empty wine bottle and empty wine glass. She was smiling. She was one hot mess.

That evening he again saw her sitting by herself at the bar, eating wings and drinking a martini. *I wonder if I can get her attention and get away from this mess. I'll buy her a drink that always seems to work.* It didn't, he barely got a smile and a wave.

When he saw her at the restaurant balcony. He just had to try again.

"Ha, ha. No. Well, yes, you so easily handled the mess, you are interesting. And it, as I said, you looked like you needed a martini. You were sitting their scowling over your notebook, kind of lost in thought. I like people who think. Oh God, you are so different from me. I'm not thinking. Sorry."

My mimosa was near its bottom. The waitress showed up, on cue, with another mimosa. Dana gestured toward my drink and said "Aloha. Can I have one of those Mimosa's. They look very good."

The waitress said yes, and as she turned away from Dana, gave me the thumbs up sign.

"Besides" Dana continued "I saw you early yesterday, and you looked like you just worked out some deep issues."

"Earlier! When? Where?" I was a bit puzzled.

"Yesterday, at about dawn. In the lobby you were very cute, all sandy, a little disheveled. Carrying an empty wine bottle and wine glass."

"Oh God." I hid my eyes.

"No, you looked great, like you just solved the problems of the world. You were smiling. Do you have a thing for dawn, wine and sand?"

"Yes." I said assertively "Yes, I have a thing for all three. Yes, I was sandy, drunk, and just watch the sun come up. But I was on a mission."

I took the discussion back to him, "You do have a thing for messy women, don't you?"

"Most definitely." Dana had spent the morning evaluating the messier parts of his relationships. He hadn't gone as far as Lisa to take up a notebook. His notebook was a bar napkin. He had jotted down a few things, a few days earlier. *Young women aren't worth the mess. Can I settle down? Can I be a better father to Alyssa? What's happiness?* And finely, *What's love?* He folded it up. It was still in his pocket.

"So, what was that mission? It must have been very important? Was it a secret mission?" He asked, smiling.

"How did you know it was a secret mission?" I let the question hang in the air. "The mission was to find myself and I succeeded. I found myself sitting on a beach in Hawaii. I walked up to myself, and we had a long talk. And finally, around dawn myself told me the secret." That was about as precise as I could put it.

"Interesting, what's the secret?"

"Well, the secret is..." I leaded forward and whispered. "I am responsible for my own happiness."

He sat and thought a bit. *Amazing! She is working down the same road I am. She's way ahead of me of course,* Dana thought. "Are you sure that No one else can make you happy?" He asked adding his own twist.

"That's not the point. It is my responsibility to be happy. To accept happiness, or reject it." I so wanted to take out my notebook, right then, and write that down.

"OK." He said, as he settled back thinking, *My God she's on the right track. How do I turn this to my advantage?* Was his next thought.

"It's really not that simple, I'm still working through all the messy parts. That's why I was unresponsive last night, no offence. I didn't want to be disturbed last night. I didn't need to be disturbed"

"And today." He said.

"And today I can buy my own mimosas, thank you very much." I said with a smile, with a little giggle.

"I would like to hear more about the messy parts." He smiled back.

"Maybe someday." I backed off. "I think now, I need to order some food." I said as I picked up my menu.

"Sounds good." He replied picking up his own menu. "What do you fancy?" He asked with a smile.

"Aloha." He called the waitress. "We would like to order two more mimosas, and Lisa what would you like to eat?"

We sat and chatted, First the obvious things, I lived in Chicago. Dana lived in Atlanta. A negative. He had a grown daughter, Alyssa, who lived in Atlanta. I had grown children, a daughter, Bridget, in L.A. and a son, Sean, in San Francisco.

Quite a while later I called for separate checks. It was well past six o'clock, actually just a few hours till sundown.

"Dana, it has been wonderful. But, now I need to enjoy some sand, ocean and a little late sun." I made ready and collected my things rising, ready to leave.

He stood as I stood, he continued. "I'm not doing anything right now." Hoping for an opening.

"Join me, if you want?" I offered.

"I thought you would never ask." Dana said.

I'm 5' 10", tall for a woman, and with 3" inch wedges I was all of 6' 1". Dana stood, Showing off his six-foot two-inch frame. For a few seconds we stood eye to eye. Blue eyes to blue eyes, only inches apart. I froze in a hypnotic trance for a moment.

From across the room, the receptionist seeing us prepare to leave, smiled.

"Excuse me." I said breaking the trance, "I need to use the lady's room." I headed off in the direction of the lady's room.

Upon, returning to the receptionist desk. The waitress stopped me, smiled, and she whispered, "See, I told you, you're too pretty to be alone for long." Giving me the 'No Problem' signal. I blushed. I really blushed. It was a total adolescent response, I knew that but still, I blushed, smiled and reaching for her hand gave it a little squeeze. I was happy. I had taken responsibility of my life, blushed, smiled and was happy.

Dana, at the front desk chatting was up the receptionist. He never miss and opportunity, it was an old habit with him. "Later," He smiled at the receptionist. He put his hand gently around my waist, "ready?"

'What is he doing? We don't even know each other," Lisa thought as Dana guided her down the steps. When they reached the street,

Lisa gently took his hand off her waist.

Reaching the sand, they sat on a bench and removed their shoes. I was wearing my new sun hat. I had my shoes, and purse in hand. Dana had only his shoes in hand.

They walked the water's edge, With the shallow waves sometime just below their knees, they enjoyed the warm Hawaiian sun, and cool Pacific waters. They started to learn more about each other.

Dana, was an art dealer. Buying and selling art to studios, interior decorators, and a few collectors. He had only one employee, his daughter.

I had a company that made very small parts for other companies. I had too many employees.

Eventually, they sat in the sand and watched the sun go down. As the last rays of light danced their last dance of the day, across the tops of the darkening waves. As the sun slid towards tomorrow, Dana again put his arm around her waist. He turned and smiled, "Hi Lisa" and lightly kissed my lips.

Lisa let the kiss linger on her lips. Then she turned her gaze out to sea. She needed a moment, to collect herself, and understand what was happening. Dana, sensing Lisa needed a few minutes, turned his gaze seaward.

"Sorry, If I mis read the signals. I thought, well, that you liked me." Dana looked down at his feet.

"I do like you, but you really don't know me." I tried to explain without giving away my secret. My hands were shaking; my whole body was quivering. I had never meant for it to go this far, especially at our first meeting.

"I see." He said disappointed

"I really liked the kiss. I haven't been kissed in a long time. A really long time, I was just a little surprised is all." I tried to explain.

Identity

I was trying to smooth over what might turn out to be an awkward moment.

We sat quietly for a few more minutes.

'Oh God what am I letting myself in for?' I thought. *'I was only trying to be a little flirtatious. Just having a little fun. Enjoying a really handsome man. Now it was moving way to fast. But what a charmer he is. I have really over played my hand.'*

Shortly, Dana stood and offered his hand to me. I took it, and after standing, let go.

With the hotel lights showing us the way along the water's edge. The sky was newly illuminated by the first evening stars, providing us with a romantic view. As we walked along the water's edge, toward our hotel, we didn't speak much. We were each lost in our own thoughts. Each of us looking into space. The stars. But also looking into ourselves. We both were thinking *What now?* From two distinct vantage points.

As we reached the hotel, Dana broke the silence. He had come to some sort of decision, and I had not. "I know of a little piano bar, down the street not very far. You might know it The Monk."

"Sorry. I've only been in Hawaii a few days. Still trying to find my way home." I stammered.

"Well, it's really nice. The piano really has a bar built around it. So you sit right at the piano. I know the guy who is playing tonight, he's a really slim black guy with a Ray Charles voice, he is awesome. The best piano player I have ever met. He knows all the really good songs. Not the new ones, the ones we know. Just the ones from over ten years ago." Dana was in for the sale. "And I really don't want to let you go, the evening is still so early."

"I really don't know, let me think about it for a few minutes." I touched his shoulder, as we reached the hotel.

The hotel provided a foot shower to wash the beach sand off our feet. Dana held the valve open while I rinsed my feet. After rinsing his own, he stepped right into his deck shoes.

I sat on a nearby bench. Shoes in hand, looking up at the stars.

"Still thinking about it?" Dana asked.

"No, just letting my feet dry." Holding up my shoes. "New shoes, I didn't want to ruin them."

"So, you're going with me?" He laughed.

Looking down, I nodded my head *yes*, and smiled.

The Monk was more bar than restaurant. It was a little full when we arrived. We ordered our martini's at the bar. We waited for a place at the piano to open up. We had just received our martini's when two seats opened at the piano bar.

Sitting ourselves comfortably, Dana tipped the piano player and asked for *Bridge Over Troubled Waters* by Paul Simon. Leaning over he said "I love that song, it means friendship over problems to me."

"Really, why?" I asked curious.

"Because, if you have a friend at your back, you'll always survive. And if you're the friend, then you need to have someone at your back." He explained.

I didn't really understand. I think he was trying to sound thoughtful.

"By the way, you smell wonderful." He complemented me on my perfume, trying to score some points. He did.

Before the song finished, Dana received a tap on the shoulder. It was the blond, Lucy, from the night before at the hotel bar. She whispered something in Dana's ear, then backed away. Studying Danas' face.

Looking around "Lucy, I'd like you to meet Lisa." Dana did the reluctant introductions.

"Hi Lisa, I'm here with my husband" gesturing to a table near the wall.

"Thanks again Dana." She said as she slipped into the crowd back towards her table.

"You were with them last night, weren't you?" I asked.

"Yes, lovers spat. I tried to help out. Looks OK now." He looked over his shoulder at the couple.

"Nice" I said. Something was up, but then again it was none of my business.

Dana suggested we move to a table on the patio, just on the other side of the piano bar. "It's easier to talk." Dana explained. I also noticed it was out of eye shot of Lucy and her husband.

"Kind of young to be married. Lucy, I mean. But who am I to talk? I was younger than her when I was married the first time." I noted.

"Yes, she's all of twenty." Dana took a deep sigh.

I decided to press, after all if Dana decided to walk, I would have less to explain and probably avoid a lot of pain. "You like them young, don't you?"

"Yes. But I'm getting too old." He said not thinking of what he was saying.

"Really can't, get...aaaa...,never mind." I stopped myself before making a mistake, and saying what I was thinking.

Looking at me a little shocked. Dana defended himself. "I can!" Thinking a bit. "But, you know young girls. They are crazy needy, too flighty, and I've got a daughter more than a few years older than her. Maybe. Not her specifically." After a few seconds "Can we order another martini?" He said as he signaled for the waiter.

137

Changing the subject, he asked. "You said earlier you were on a mission. It sounded like you were seeking happiness."

"Yes, to get away, and well, find...more like figure out what would make me happy. Or, you know what could make me happy. Well, you know." Thinking a second. "More like why I'm not happy. Kind of." I continued. " What I did figure out by sunrise, is that I'm responsible. At least that's a step forward."

"Well, I've been thinking about that today." Dana offered.

"Just today. Don't let it hurt your head, it will pass." I was kind of offended. I had been working on the question of happiness for months.

"No, I guess it's been in the back of my head, mind. No, it's really Alyssa fault. She's been after me to "grow up!"

"And you don't want to grow up?" I smiled.

"I don't know how." Dana said.

"The nice thing about being a grown up is that you don't have to grow up! You just have to be responsible." There it was again 'responsibility'. "Responsible for your own happiness." I quoted my mantra.

"Kind of heavy for a first date." Dana answered.

"Oh, so were on a date?" I was a little shocked.

"Sure. I asked, you accepted. Remember?" Dana put it back at me.

God he's fast and a lot smarter than I gave him credit for. "Yes, I accepted."

"One more martini. If that's OK?' Dana asked.

We sat and listen to *Fool on the Hill*. We let the lyrics sink into our semi-conscious mind.

Identity

As we finished our martini's and began to make ready to leave. Dana leaned over and gave me a soft kiss on the lips. This time I said thank you.

We walked back to the hotel hand in hand. In the lobby, I turned to say good night.

"I'll walk you safely to your room." Dana said, As I began to decline "You never know what kind of people might be staying here." He warned.

"You're staying here!" I noted.

"Exactly!" He smiled.

I laughed a little "OK, just to my door, not through my door, outside my door, got it?"

"Yes my lady, got it."

My mind was spinning. No way. I'm not doing it, he doesn't know me, doesn't know about me. I'm not filling in the blanks, no sir, not tonight.

When we reached the door, I took the key card out of my purse, and holding it tightly in my hand, put my hand behind my back.

"I had a wonderful time. I enjoy your company very much. You're an interesting and charming man." I said "But this is as far as you go." Holding my hat and purse in one hand and the key card tightly behind my back.

"I fully understand. No problem. But may I have a good night kiss?"

"I thought you would never ask." I stepped a little closer.

He put both hands on my waist and pulled me close to his body. He then gave me a long, slow, wet, passionate kiss, as he pulled me tight to his body. My mind went blank. I dropped my purse and hat. He had sucked the air out of my lungs, leaving me standing there in a daze, gazing up to where he had been. He politely picked up my hat and purse. Giving me a smile, and a little bow and said. "Good night. May I see you tomorrow?"

"Aah, sure." Was all I could manage, and gave him a little good bye wave.

He turned and headed for the elevators. I watch him go. I also admired what I saw, for about a half a minute. Sighing, I open my door.

WOW my mind said, then I mouthed the word *WOW*, then finally the words came out, "WOW".

What the hell am I getting myself into, I wondered as I prepared for bed. *I'm not ready for this, whatever this is. I'm just finding myself. Never mind. I will probably never see him again. Just like all the other Romeo's who have popped in and out of my life.*

Even if he wanted me, big if. He might even be disgusted by me, as I have been told. "I'm disgusted by you" I can still hear the words.

So, I took a long sigh before thinking *I took responsibility for my own happiness today. And I was happy. It was my decision. All else is behind me.*

DRIVER, I'M CHANGING DIRECTION

Chapter 16

It was 7:30 a.m. I was adapting to the time change. It only took thirty-six hours without sleep plus two more days. But I was getting close to my normal wake up time.

I lay with the pillow over my head, hoping its soft and squishy insides would protect me from the real world for just a little longer. My eyes were protected, but not my memory. I was on a date! I haven't been on a real date for months and months. And that date didn't go well. This one did! And it was worth waiting for. Even if it wasn't like a real date where they call you and ask you out for another night, just so you can daydream about it, try on different outfits, get all made up. But it *was* a date.

Throwing my pillow across the bed, it fell on the floor. *Okay, girl, out of bed. It's a new day.*

I used the toilet, made coffee, grabbed my notebook, and finally got comfortable in my overstuffed chair on the balcony.

Looking over, I noticed the strappy chair I placed in the room still had the note on it from the day before.

I opened my notebook. *Okay. The question was can anyone else make you happy? I'm responsible. So I can accept it or reject it. So can the people on my list accept or reject?* "Chilling thought," I said aloud.

Okay. Me first. I wrote on my own page. *Can I accept being called disgusting?* I did accept it, and I've carried it with me ever since.

The messy part is I didn't know at the time that I could and should have rejected being called disgusting. So now it bled through makeup, clothing, success, failure, pain, and pleasure. I realized may have to go back to that person someday and say, "No, I reject that. I am not disgusting!" I wrote that down.

I was lost in thought for over two and a half hours. It was after ten and still no call from Dana. I felt my spirit sinking. *No. I reject that. His problems are not mine.*

I need to get out of this room, I thought as I headed off to the bathroom. I had taken off my T-shirt and panties and had just turned on the shower when the phone rang. I shut off the shower and picked up the phone on the bathroom wall.

"Yes," I answered.

***

The impact of the day's events, ideas, promises, and problems lay on Dana's pillow well into the morning hours. Dana got up around 5:00 a.m. as usual and made his phone call. After the phone call, he just sat sipping coffee, thinking about Lisa. *She's different. I don't know how. I can't put my finger on it. But I like her.*

Before going into the bathroom, he took his bar napkin out of his pants pocket. He read it again. Then using a bit of toothpaste, he stuck it to the mirror. After his shower, while shaving, he read it over and over again. "What's happiness? What's love?" He asked aloud.

Wearing just a towel around his waist, standing in the middle of his room, Dana made a decision. A few minutes later he called the front desk to make reservations. *I hope Lisa is up*, he thought as he dialed her room.

"Hi, this is Dana. Are you up?"

"Sure. I have been for a while," Lisa said.

"I've reserved a table with an umbrella, on the patio, with a view of the ocean. I've ordered mimosas for eleven thirty. Would you like to join me?

***

"Sure," I said as casually as I could. "What time was that again?" Like I didn't know.

"Eleven thirty."

"Okay, I've got a few things I need to do. So I'll aim for eleven-thirty. What time is it now?"

"It's ten-twenty now."

"I might be a little late, so..."

"No problem," Dana said, adding, "I'll see yea when you get there. Aloha."

"Bye." I hung up.

Looking in the mirror Lisa thought, *Oh, sure that's easy for you to say. Sure no problem,* as she shrugged her shoulders. *I've only got an hour and ten minutes to make myself look beautiful.* "Well, I'd better get to work." She said aloud.

In the lobby, I saw my friend Porter. "Aloha. How is your day?" I said.

"Aloha," he said as he turned toward me. "Oh, just another day in paradise, talking to a beautiful woman."

"Okay, who is that?" I asked, looking around.

"Oh, Miss Lisa, you of course." Porter was very good at flattery.

"Porter, I need sunglasses. Nice ones and quick. Can you help me?"

"In the hotel shop to your right, we have sunglasses. A little pricey. I'll admit, but convenient, or..."

"No, convenient and quick is what I need. Thank you." I turned and took a few steps and turned around in mid step, looking back. I asked, "Am I supposed to say aloha when I leave?"

"Always appropriate," Porter agreed.

"Aloha." I smiled and waved.

***

I made my entrance, seemingly unhurried, and only about ten minutes late.

Dark sunglass covered his eyes from the probing rays of the noon day Hawaiian sun. A white cotton shirt covered his chest; knee length short pants completed the image. The table was set with an ice bucket, holding a bottle of champagne, also a carafe of orange juice and a plate of fresh fruit.

"Hi." I tried to think of something cute to say, but nothing came to mind. Dana stood and turned toward me.

"Aloha, Lisa," he said as he came forward and leaned in to give me a kiss. I turned my head and offered him my cheek. No performance like last night.

"You smell nice," Dana commented as he pulled out a chair for me.

Dana poured some orange juice into a champagne flute and topped it off with champagne. He then offered me some fruit.

I thanked him for the night before, then we chatted about the bar, how great the music was and how good the piano player was. We did everything we could to avoid the truths about Lucy and previous lives.

About an hour later, his cell phone rang. "Aloha, Alyssa. How you doing, sweetie?"

"Just sitting by the ocean with my new best friend, Lisa." He said as he winked at me. Dana listened for a few seconds. "Oh shit, I forgot! I know. Text me the details. I know. Okay, sweetie. Love you." He put down his cell phone and turned to me. "I forgot all

144

about this thing." *This isn't bad,* Dana thought. *This will give me a chance to impress her. Maybe get to know her better, and who knows?* "How would you like to go to an art gallery exhibit this evening with me?" He asked.

"An art exhibit?"

"Yes, there is an artist here in Hawaii, who has become very popular in Atlanta. I have a client who wants some pieces. It wasn't my original mission, but it came up a few days ago."

"So, you have to work, and you want me to tag along?" I asked.

"No, no. It's not like that. It's fun. I know the dealer, and he goes all out for these things. Please."

"So, I wander around, looking at art, drinking wine, and eating hors d'oeuvres while you are in a back room somewhere negotiating the price of a piece of art?"

"No, well yes. But it only takes fifteen minutes or so," Dana said.

"Did I say that was a bad thing? Take your time." I put my hand under my chin in a seductive way. "Excuse me, handsome. Do you think this might be Hawaiian primitive art. Are you married?" I added as a little dig.

"Ten minutes, that is all the time you have to seduce someone else. After all, you already seduced me," Dana said with a smile.

Well, I didn't expect that. No one has tried to seduce me in quite a while. I better change the subject. I then asked, "Is this hoity-toity?" Dana gave me a puzzled look.

"Hoity-toity, you know, jackets for men and cocktail dresses for women?" I added.

"I guess, I don't know. I'm wearing a tan slacks, a white shirt, and blue blazer." He stumbled. "I have to look in control."

"In control of?" I teased.

"The negotiations." Dana said with a wink.

"Well, you're going to look fabulous and formidable," I added, thinking that at six-four, he would be very formidable.

"Hoity-toity it is then. What time?" I asked.

"Around six o'clock. I'll pick you up." Dana answered as he settled back in his chair. "I know where you live." Dana smiled.

"Okay. What time is it now?"

"About twelve thirty." As he checked his cell phone for the time. I started putting a list together in my head. The longer I sat there, the longer the list got. I casually sipped my mimosa. I figured I had to leave in about thirty minutes, so it didn't seem that I was in a panic; but I was.

"There will be appetizers and cocktails," Dana added. "Yes, you said that." I said

"I'll make reservations at a hoity-toity restaurant for afterward. My new word for the day, 'hoity-toity,'" he continued.

Thirty minutes later, I sipped the last of my mimosa. As I rose up, I said. "I've got a few things to do, so I'll see you at six. Aloha."

In the lobby, I looked for Porter. *Where are you?* I thought, as a bit of panic rose in my throat. Then I saw him standing by the street side door. "Porter! Aloha, Porter. Please help me." I quickly moved on before he could talk. "I need a manicure and a pedicure and quick! Where is a good place?" I was sure he knew everything.

"I'll call my sister," he said. "She'll know."

I gave him a hug, as I stepped into the taxi. "Thank you so much, Porter. Aloha."

146

By four thirty, I was back at the hotel. By six, I was powered, painted, and dressed. Sitting back for a second, I started thinking, *How did the gods of Nordstrom know I was going to need this scarlet cocktail dress and matching shoes.* They were perfect. *Except, why didn't I get a matching clutch?*

Neither of my two purses was right. Shit. I looked around. My cell phone case is red! Not a matching scarlet but red. I took the cell phone out. It was still off. I stuffed in my driver's license, hotel key card, a credit card and a few dollars; no room for much else.

I stood in the middle of the room. *Nothing left to do. I'm all done up.* I checked myself in the mirror for the fifteenth time. I'm about as girl as a girl can be.

Have I thought this through? I've been rushed, and I've been so happy. No. I haven't. Is it too late to back out? Knock at the door. Too late.

***

Shutting the door behind me, Dana said, "Wow, breathtaking."
"I bet you say that to all your dates, but it's a nice line. Does it ever work?" I asked.

"I don't know first time I used it. Did it work?" He asked.

"Kind of." I added in the elevator, "But I know you have used it before. Did it work?"

Dana blushed a little and didn't answer.

In the taxi, Dana put his hand lightly on my knee. "Thank you for coming tonight. I hate going to these things alone."

"My pleasure. I've never been to soiree like this." My nervous heart began its inevitable journey from its rightful resting place, up through my throat to just below my tongue, often preventing me from speech. Public gatherings like this always seemed risky.

Dana took my hand and walked me into the gallery. As we entered, Dana scanned the gallery, studying the layout and taking note of the attendees.

As we stood in the entry way, several men took note of the tall redhead in the scarlet mini dress. A comment, "Great legs," drifted my way from a man dressed in a black shirt with a white collar and cuffs and a black tie. He was no priest.

Someone called out, "Dana, here!"

"Hi, Congressman." Dana led me through the crowd. "Carl, I'd like you to meet Lisa."

"Happy to meet you, Lisa." Then to Dana, "Your taste in women has improved."

Dana looked at me. "Greatly," he said, making me blush.

We drifted around the room, sipping champagne and tasting the hors d'oeuvres. I enjoyed the art; Dana studied it.

We chatted with the artist and several patrons of the arts. Few were locals.

At one point, Dana felt he had enough information and excused himself, leaving me in the care of the congressman.

No sooner had Dana left, the man in the black shirt and black tie approached us. "Hi, Congressman, how's DC treating you?"

"Just fine, Paul. And how's court treating you?"

Paul reached for my hand. "And who is this lovely lady, Carl?"

"Paul, I'd like you to meet Lisa. Lisa, Paul. Lisa, be careful. He's an attorney."

Paul, said handing me his card. "What brings you to this shindig?"

"Oh, I've never been to one of these shindigs. I came with Dana. I find it quite interesting and really neat."

"Well. Nice to meet you, Lisa. I hope to see you again. Congressman, nice to see you again." Then to me Paul said. "Lisa, I have to mingle, there are more felons here than you can imagine." As he left, his hand cupped my butt. I guess that's what attorneys do. Dana returned in about fifteen minutes, all smiles. We made small talk with the congressman and a few other minor celebrities for the next half hour. Dana then suggested that we leave for the hoity-toity restaurant where he had made reservation.

This was the part that I was now dreading. Dana clearly had a physical interest in me. And I was more than interested in him. But I was not as I appeared and now I had to tell Dana. This is where they usually run screaming into the night. Not really, well only once, maybe twice.

In the taxi, I gathered myself up. I worked up all the courage I could muster. "Dana, I need, I mean really need to have a discussion with you about...about the real me."

"The real you? Are you a spy? On a secret mission? You told me that yesterday." Dana was still being the dapper seducer.

"Please don't be so damn charming. This is serious, and hard for me," I pleaded.

"Okay. What?' He asked.

"I'm sorry. Can we go to that park bench we were at the other day, the one on the beach?" I pleaded.

Dana simply sat a second, saw that I was serious, and said, "Driver, change course," and gave him directions. As we reached the bench Dana said, "So, we're here."

"Dana, I really, really like you. You're handsome, smart, capable, funny, charming. I could go on, and on. And I so respect you, but I have not been completely honest with you. I haven't been completely honest with myself either. And I really, really, don't understand why you have taken an interest in me," I began.

149

"Well—" Dana started. "Shhh," I quieted him.

Dana looked directly into my eyes. He did not smile, only intense concentration.

"I didn't intend for it to go this far." I started, taking a deep breath. Bracing myself for whatever happens next.

"Dana, I'm a pre-op transsexual. I started out as a boy, now I'm a woman. These are not my breasts, just silicon bags under my skin. My soon-to-be lady parts, my vagina, the doctors will make it out of my penis. I'll have the final surgery is in less than two weeks, in Phoenix. It, my new vagina, will work. I mean it will be useful. I will be able to have climaxes. I've been getting surgeries. The doctors operated on me more than once. But I'm not a complete woman. I'm sorry, I really am."

I waited in silence, arms folded, head down; it seemed like years. "How long have you been a woman?" Dana asked. "I'm not sure that's the right question or maybe it is. How about how long have you been having surgeries?'

"Over a year," I whispered.

"I had the breasts implanted over five years ago," I quietly added. "I've been passing as a woman long before that."

"But I've always felt like a woman," I said looking up "I kind of feel like I was just having corrective surgery."

Dana looked out to sea, then up at the stars. "I'm not gay."

"I know." I said, feeling the world coming apart, beginning with my heart. "I know." I said again.

"I'm not gay, Lisa." His hand rubbed his forehead.

"If it's worth anything." My voice shaking more than my soul. "I don't feel like I'm gay ether. That's why I'm having the surgery. So I can be a woman. The woman that I am."

Dana shook his head. "I don't understand, I'm not gay. Hell, I'm anything, but gay. I don't understand."

I saw myself beginning to disintegrate, dissolving into the sand, a human sandcastle being torn down and made invisible in the sand by waves and waves of pain. As my chest became hollowed out, my heart and lungs dissolving, all I could say was "I'm so sorry, I didn't intend; I'm so sorry, I didn't intend for it to go this far. I'm so sorry."

I stood and backed away then turned and ran. I ran down the beach. The lights leading my way blurred as I passed by. When I could run no more, I fell to my knees in the sand. I looked up at the stars. "Phony. Fake. Disgusting," the stars called down to me.

My shoulders collapsed into my sides. My disgusting body weighed a thousand pounds. I staggered like a drunken woman down the beach. Reaching the hotel, I didn't bother with the foot bath. I stopped and looked at it, remembering being happy. I walked barefoot across the lobby, head down.

As I entered my room, I threw down my key card, shoes, and phone case clutch. Then I lock and bolted the door. In the bathroom, I took the ceramic cover off the tissue box. Pulling out numerous tissues, I wiped my eyes and nose. Carrying it with me, I sat down on the bed.

I could not sit. I stood and paced, sat on the bed again. I put the tissue box on the nightstand and paced again. Finally, I came to rest in the balcony doorway, leaning against the door frame using it support my body made heavy by my heart.

My stare was as blank as my soul. Only my tears reminded me I had a heart.

A knock at the door pulled me back from the dark ocean horizon.

Stepping to the door, I looked out the peephole. Dana! I turned and leaned against the door. A knock again, and Dana called, "Lisa, please."

I was no longer in possession of any understanding of what I was doing.

I open the door with the slid lock on. "Yes."

"Lisa, please listen to me. Can we talk?"

"I guess." I said keeping the slid lock on, speaking through the crack between the frame and the door.

"Please, I'm not going to hurt you. Please can I talk to you?"

"Second," I called, shutting the door. I checked myself in the bathroom mirror. "Oh God," I whispered. I wiped off as much mascara as possible. Picking up my key card, I back off the slid lock and took a deep breath. I guess I asked for it.

I opened the door and stepped out, shutting the door behind me. In my bare feet, standing before Dana, I was struck at how much taller than I he was.

Dana took a step back giving me some space. "Can we go someplace to talk?"

Without a word, I walked down the hall to the elevator waiting area. In any other hotel in any other place in the US, there would be a large window. Not here in Hawaii, just a window sill, no glass, just view. A wonderful view of the darken sky and ocean.

I pulled the bench out from the wall, making room for me to lean against the sill. Looking out at the sky and ocean, I let the night breeze brush my hair back.

Dana came around the bench, standing next to me. His hands were folded on the sill. He took a deep breath.

"Sex is important, not just for satisfying the sensory glands.

But for a complete giving of one's self. The intimate knowledge of sharing, but that is not why I'm interested in you, taken by you really."

I broke in, "Dana, I will be able to have sex. I will just have to be careful."

"Oh, that's great." He pushed on.

"As I was saying," Dana said, "I only know you as a woman, as a very attractive, intelligent, feminine, sensual woman. That is the way I'll always know you. I don't want to know the other you. The one that's going away." Dana took another deep breath. "I mean I want to get to know you better. Something in you, in us, is drawing us closer together. So it doesn't matter. You're more than your body. You are more than a woman. You are unique and fascinating. And I do want to get to know you better."

"I don't know why you are interested in me." I started. "I think you have to let what I told you sink in." I waited

Dana sat down on the bench. I turned and faced him. He said, "I was never attracted to men." Dana thought a minute "But you're a woman, a classy woman. More woman than any woman I have ever met. So I..."

"Dana, in a few weeks, what's left of this." I said gesturing toward my crotch. "Will be gone." Taking a second. "So you can walk away still thinking of me as a woman. The woman I am trying very hard to be."

Dana looked over at me "I don't want to walk away."

"Then, what do you want to do?" I asked and I held my breath.

"I don't know, I really don't know." He contemplated. "I'm being honest here; I'm just attracted to you. I think you are the most interesting woman I ever met. So I just want to see where it goes from here." And after a few seconds "Just that."

"Well, I'm interested also. I would like to see where it goes." I said.

After a few silent minutes went by with me trying to study his face to try and figure out what he was thinking. Finally, to at least move things along, I said, "I know you're thinking lots of things. Let it out. What do you want to know? I'll answer every question honestly. From now on out, only honesty. I tell you anything you want to know." I thought for a second. "Have you ever known a transsexual?"

"No, I haven't." He continued, "How do you have sex? I mean I've never been with a..."

"I think the words you're looking for is pre-op transsexual. Don't say gay." I went on, "I don't have sex with men, not now at least. Now, I'm more of a pleaser." I answered, "At least 'til after the final surgery."

"Why again have you...have you changed? Did you change to be with a man?"

"No, I changed because I always felt I was a woman. I like being a woman. But as a woman, I want to be complete. I want to be a complete woman."

Dana thought for a second. "Why don't you want to be a man?"

"That's easy. I know them to well," I began. "I was one once remember? Besides, I don't like stubble. I like smooth legs. I don't like body hair. I like long hair. I like the way perfume smells on me. I like pretty clothes and high heels. I like being treated like a lady and all that implies. And during sex, I like to be the woman."

"And you always felt this way?" Dana asked.

"Always since I can remember. Anything else?" I asked

Dana shook his head no. He didn't look up.

"Okay. I'm tired, and I'm sure you're exhausted," I said. Dana stood and, taking my hand, walked me to my door. I held the key card tightly in my hand and placed it behind my back, just like the night before.

Dana didn't say a thing. He just put his hands around my waist and pulled me close to him. He slowly leaned in and gave me one of those long, passionate kisses, and as he did, both hands slid to my butt cheeks, grasping them firmly, pulling me to his body. I could feel his chest against me and his hips against mine. His right hand moved up to my breast; he didn't squeeze. He caressed it gently. The kiss lasted forever and not long enough.

As Dana released me, he took a step back. He just kept looking into my eyes for an answer to his unasked question. I took a deep breath. "It's now or never," I thought. I took my hand from behind my back. I held out my hand and offered him my key card.

"Would you like to open my door?"

WHAT NOW, MISTER?

Chapter 17

Ever since my first surgery, quite frankly, I have been afraid of sex! So when we got in the room, I didn't know exactly what to do. So I decided to be the woman I am in as many ways as possible.

I had not been naked, completely naked, in front of anyone, including my doctors, since my last marriage. I still was not ready to be seen naked. I excused myself to put on my sexy silk negligee.

So after I pleasured Dana over several hours, I fell into a deep peaceful sleep until 5:00 a.m. When Dana jumped out of bed and leapt into his pants and shirt, I was wide awake, but I feigned that I was a sleep. He leaned over and gave me a kissed on the forehead. He whispered, "Later," and carrying his shoes he quietly slipped out the door.

I sat up in bed, shaking my head. I wasn't happy. "A kiss on the forehead for God's sake," I said out loud. I looked at the clock: five-o-five for God's sake, and he races out the door. Throwing myself back down on the bed, I tensed every muscle in my body then, kicking and pounding the bed, let out an "Auggggggaugg!" And more than a few shits.

I rolled out of bed and headed toward the bathroom. I stopped at the full length mirror. Dropping my negligee to the floor, I stood looking at my naked self. I thought, *Shit! Who wouldn't run away from this?* Then I asked myself aloud, "What did I do wrong this time? I always do something wrong. I'm always to blame." Tears formed. "What did I do?"

Through tears of humiliation and shame, I searched the floor for my panties and T-shirt. I turned away from the mirror and put them on, covering the offending parts of my body. I thought, *He probably thinks I'm disgusting. I don't blame him. I've been told "You're disgusting" before.*

I automatically picked up my notebook and pen then made my way to my friendly overstuffed chair on the balcony. *Why did I do this? Am I just stupid to think someone would want me?* I just sat there watching the sun leave the ocean for the red and orange sky. I looked up. "Oh, you again, but you are so lovely the way you kiss my face, warm my soul. I wish you were my man. If you would have me. Do I disgust you? Will you burn me?" I looked down at the notebook. I started a page for Dana and started writing. I couldn't help but write under his name. *What did I do wrong?* It never came to my mind that Dana could have done anything wrong. It's always my fault. I wrote, *Love.* Scratched it out. I sat for a second then threw the notebook across the deck. I sobbed for a full five minutes before making my way back to the notebook. "Sorry," I said aloud to the notebook as I picked it up.

Taking a deep breath, I said, "Okay, stop it. Get a hold of yourself, girl. I am the girl. I should write that down." Again, I was talking aloud to my notebook. It was becoming a habit. I wrote down on my page, *I am the girl.* I should think about that. How does my becoming a girl have to do with how it will affect my loved ones, even the ones who don't love me? I need to understand how I will change things. "Me, how will I change things? No one else is changing, just me. It's all my fault." I said out loud again to the notebook. I wrote that down.

I was in the fog of writing and trying to understand what I was writing when the phone gained my attention on about the fifth ring.

Slipping out of my chair, I looked at the clock on my way to the phone. How did it get to be after nine o'clock?

***

As soon as Dana reached his room, he organized his call to Alyssa. The call only took about twenty minutes; that gave him enough time to sit on his balcony, sip coffee, and think. "God knows that I've done more thinking in the last few days than I have in years about myself and my future," he whispered to his coffee.

The last few days were all puzzle pieces all scattered around the room. As he thought about it, the pieces seemed to work themselves together. Now, he was getting the picture, a bit psychedelic and not very clear. All full of colors and strange lines and angles but, nonetheless, a picture; perhaps a picture of the future?

Lisa was one hell of a woman, he thought, regardless. Fooled him, not to mention a congressman and prominent playboy attorney. *Wow, last night. Wow. No gay about that. He had never been taken care of that way by any woman he had ever known.* He thought aloud, "I don't care if they are plastic. Those are some great tits." *She said that soon she'll have her final operation. Then she'll have a vagina. A new vagina.* "Wait, that makes her a virgin. Well, that's hot," he said out loud to himself again.

He called and set up a fancy brunch then called Lisa.

***

I answered the phone on the bed stand. "Did I wake you?" Dana asked.

Sitting down on the unmade bed, I was not sure of where that was going. I wasn't sure why he was calling. I really didn't know what to say. So I coldly said, "No, I've been up for quite a while."

"Good," Dana said, not reading the tone in my voice. "I've reserved a table for us on the top floor restaurant. They have a

159

great brunch here and a sea view. It's really lovely. This time for ten thirty, is that okay?"

"Second," I said as I turned my head and grabbed a tissue and blew my nose. I needed to take a few second to collect myself.

"Lisa, is everything okay?" He asked, now reading the stress in my voice.

"A second please!" I said a bit harshly then "Sorry, I'm in the middle of something. Give me a second, okay?" I said in a softer, more feminine tone.

"Sure," Dana said and then sat silently. He wasn't sure what was happening, but it was clear he didn't need to say a thing.

After everything I put myself through this morning. My fault again. Do I just want to put myself out there to be hurt again? Well, I guess the hard part is over. He knows me, all about me. At least the top half. And he did call me, asking for a date. Can I chance it? I made my decision "Of course. I would love to," I said, smiling into the phone giving a little laugh. I hung up, wondering *how the hell am I going to keep this emotional roller coaster on the tracks? I keep getting flung from one side to the other; up then down then up again. What a mess.*

I cleaned myself up as best I could. I dressed as I had that first day at the Bagatelle restaurant and with no bra. *When was that yesterday? The day before last week? I don't know, and I'm not going to stop and figure it out.* I hurried to my shower. I was in the lobby by ten twenty.

Seeing Porter, I called, "Aloha," and quickly moved toward him and gave him a big hug.

"Well, Aloha to you too," he said with a little surprised look on his face.

"Thank you, thank you and please." I said showing my nails. "Thank your sister Keri also. She's a godsend. Aloha."

Identity

"Have a wonderful day, Lisa, Aloha," he called out as I walked to an express roof-top elevator.

***

Dana had a taken a table next to the Hawaiian-style window, again no glass. The white sun was just gaining control over the Earth and oceans, shading the ocean in spectrum of blue shades. The palm trees creating hiding places from the suns prying rays.

I came up behind him. I put my arms around his neck and gave him a kiss on the cheek. "Aloha."

Dana stood up and gave me a kiss on the lips.

"Well, I like the way you say aloha." I smiled. Dana sat me down and poured me a mimosa. After a few silent seconds that seemed like minutes, I asked, "Why did you run out on me at 5:00 a.m. this morning?"

"I'm sorry if I woke you up. I tried to be quite." Not answering my question.

"Not the answer I was looking for," I said directly with a little pout.

"I was scheduling with Alyssa and then a conference call with a dealer organization. It didn't last very long. It's part of my work, and it comes off at 5:30 a.m. Hawaiian time. That's 1:30 p.m. Atlanta time. Sometimes it lasts a few hours and sometimes three or four hours. I never know," Dana explained as he quietly sipped his mimosa.

"Oh, work," I said, just then realizing it was Wednesday evening in Chicago. *Work was not part of my notebook. Paula was but work wasn't. Oh God, I was so worried about finding myself that I forgot all about work and Paula.*

Dana looked over at me. "You're mighty quiet?"

"I was just thinking of work," I said.

"I promise, no big art exhibition today," Dana said, thinking I was speaking of his work.

"No, no. I liked it, I had fun. I got to chat up a congressman. And as a bonus, I got the card of a prominent attorney," I teased. Maybe it was a good thing to get away from work, unscheduled.

Maybe. I do miss Paula, I thought.

"We can have the whole day to ourselves if you like." Dana continued.

I smiled and just said, "Yes. That would be great."

After a second I asked, "Honey, can I call you honey? If you don't like it, I won't?"

"Yes. I like," Dana said.

"Honey." I had to stop and think about how I was going to say this. "Humm," I cleared my throat "Honey. So how would you critique last night?"

"Well, it was usual. Just about what I would expect to find in Hawaii. Her technique is excellent, if not a bit common. All in all, a good artist."

I lightly scratched his arm with my new nails.

"Silly, you know what I mean. How was I?" Lisa asked with great interest.

"An excellent date. That scarlet dress was Din-O-Mite! Everyone wanted to meet you. You were the tallest most beautiful woman at the gallery or, for that matter, anywhere," Dana said.

"You'll say anything to flatter me. It really is not necessary. But, that's not what was I after. The sex part. Did I put you off? Did I ask you to do things you didn't want to do?"

"Hell no!"

"Wait. Did I do things you didn't want me to do? Be serious now." I waited for an answer.

My mind was whirling around; he had never been with anyone like me. He had never been with a woman...to be.

He waited a second, thinking. Then he reached over and took my hand. "It was a perfect night. You were more exciting in bed than any one or two women could ever be."

"Now you want two women?" I said, half in jest.

"No. Just you. You're exciting and adventuresome. Okay now, how was I?" He said throwing the question throwing it back in my face.

I waited a second and placed my middle finger between my lips and licked it. Giving him some dreamy eyes. "Best ever."

Dana blushed.

I think it's easier for the woman to ask the kinky questions, so I did. "Now that we have settled that, can I ask you a few kinky questions? Easy questions for now."

"Kinky? Okay, like how?" Dana was puzzled. See, it's always easier for me to ask.

"I like ropes and handcuffs. You know, a little light bondage. What about you?" Letting that hang in the air. "And I like vibrators. Oh, and a little light spanking when I've been a bad girl."

"Good to know," a blushing Dana said.

I sat back and sipped my mimosa. I could see he was considering the kinky side of me. "You know, by allowing you to tie me up, I'm putting a great deal of trust in you. I would have never let my first wife tie me up. Actually, now only you," I said.

I sealed the deal by leaning forward, showing major size C-plus cleavage. Dana's eyes went right where I wanted them. I pulled my tank top down just a bit, using my arms to press the kittens together; in the process, my nipples hardened.

"Oh God. Please don't do that." Dana said fidgeting.

"Why?" I asked in a low voice as I started to play with my middle finger with my tongue again.

"Because you make me so horny. I want to just jump over this table and rip your bra off."

"I'm not wearing one honey." As I pulled my tank top down a little more.

Looking around at the other tables, he said, "You're asking for it, you know."

"No, I'm begging for it." I panted as I leaned further across the table, showing even more cleavage.

Dana practically flew out of his chair. He reached down and pulled me out of my chair. Putting his arm around my waist, he walked me toward the elevator.

"You know, you deserve to be spanked for this," Dana said as we walked off, squeezing my butt.

"Yes, sir," I said as demurely as possible. "Do you have ropes?" He asked.

"No, but I have several scarves that will work," I teased.

Passing through the lobby, Porter smiled and discreetly turned away.

In the elevator, I took out my key card; handing it to Dana, I said, "You'll need this."

THAT WENT BETTER THAN I THOUGHT

Chapter 18

At 3:38 p.m. Thursday afternoon, Dana propped up on one elbow, letting one finger circle around my nipple. "Let's go to that hoity-toity restaurant. I'll make the reservations. Okay beautiful? Can I call you beautiful?

"Oh God. How did you get so charming? I've asked you that right?" I said, smiling.

"Just speaking the truth," Dana said. With his right hand going up in the air like "what?"

"Okay, just keep it to a minimum in public," I begged.

"Why? I'm just saying what everyone is thinking" was Dana's defense.

"Stop!" I said, putting my arms around Dana's neck and pulling Dana on top of me.

A long while later, Dana said, "Hoity-toity?"

"Sure, but I only have that one cocktail dress. The one I had on last night," I said.

"Fabulous, my favorite dress on or off you. I'll see you in a bit." Jumping out of bed, Dana dressed and headed for the door. Opening the door he turned toward me "See you beautiful."

***

I showered and cleaned up. I had put on my dress and had my hair held back with a head band. I was painting my face with colors and potions from various jars, compacts, and pencils when I heard the knock on the door.

Stepping around the corner, I let Dana in. "Hi, beautiful. Ready yet?" He asked before kissing my lips.

"Oh God, not yet. Sit down. Watch TV." I gestured to the strappy chair. "I won't be much longer."

After a few minutes, Dana said, "Hummm, taking a little while, are we?"

"Shut up. You're a natural beauty, I have to make it up with makeup. Get it?" I laughed at my own joke.

Shortly thereafter, I blew my hair out and slipped on my pumps before presenting myself. "Ta da!"

"Nummy. Can I have dessert now?" Dana grabbed my waist.

"Hoity first, toity later," I said, releasing myself and grabbing my chic cell phone purse.

Porter met us in the lobby with an "Aloha! Did you have a good day?"

"Excellent, outstanding, best day ever." Dana smiled and reached to hold my hand. "Now, we're off to an excellent restaurant."

"Right this way," Porter said as he headed for the door and whistled for a cab. "Aloha," Porter said as the cab left the curb.

The restaurant was just that hoity and toity, and it was nearly full. We were going to have to wait for a table. Dana guided me into the bar, seeing just one seat left at the bar. Dana turned it around so it faced out and offered me the seat. I sat and crossed my legs, showing as much leg as possible. We ordered sidecar cocktails.

A few moments later, the art dealer tapped Dana on the shoulder. "Dana, lovely to see you so soon. But last night, you failed to introduce me to this lovely lady."

"Achmed, I'm pleased to introduce Miss Lisa Wynn." Achmed bowed, took my hand, and gave it a kiss.

"I'm so very pleased to meet you," he said. Achmed looked exactly like Sydney Greenstreet. Considering the restaurant, Achmed, and his chivalry, the sidecars seemed so old world, like out of the movie Casablanca. Still, I was loving it. I started to wonder if Captain Louis, played by Claude Rains, was going to show up. And sure enough, the congressman approached our growing group.

First, he greeted me taking my hand. "I'm so happy to see you again, Lisa. I enjoyed our conversation last night so much. You gave me some things to think about concerning bringing business to our little state." Then he shook hands with Achmed, and he gave of all things a fist bump to Dana.

We had conversed for a few minutes when the attorney, Paul, from last night joined the group, cocktail in hand. "Hi you all. This is turning into quite a party," Paul said as he maneuvered himself to my side. Placing his cocktail on the bar, he turned to group and joined the conversation. After a sip or two of his cocktail, he placed his hand lightly on my thigh.

Dana visibly stiffened, and looking around, said, "I think our table is ready." It was wishful thinking on Dana's part. After taking my hand, helping me from the bar stool Dana continued, "So if you'll excuse us. It was great to see you all again. Achmed, tomorrow, we will get together and work out payment packing and shipping, okay?" We then made our way to the maître d's stand. Our table was indeed ready.

On the way to the table, I quietly asked, "Are you jealous of Paul?"

"No." He said, giving me a scowl. "Well yes, I guess I was kind of jealous. It's a new experience for me. I don't think I have ever been jealous before, or at least not for a long, long time."

"Just so you know, honey, in reference to Paul's hand on my leg; which I could see upset you. I only have thighs for you!" I laughed again at my own joke.

"Beautiful and funny. That's why I'm falling in love with you," Dana said.

Oh wow, now that I've heard the word "love," I'm not sure I'm ready for it. Things are moving way too fast. I thought of my notebook, the part where I wrote about meeting Dana. A wild roller coaster ride, being slammed left to right up and down and up again. *How am I going to keep this thing on the tracks?* I wondered. *Is that what I had written about just yesterday? Or was it this morning? See, way too fast.* I thought I needed to study my notebook. *What does it say? Accept or reject, or change the conditions?*

Dana had gone on to another topic, something about the congressman and plans for the next day. My face paid attention with the appropriate, "sure," "yes," "of course," etc., but my mind was trying to absorb what Dana had just said. *Did Dana mean it? Was it just off the cuff? Was it because we had wild sex? Would Dana say it tomorrow, in a week, in a month?* A month was about as far ahead as I wanted to think. Any further, I didn't want to think about. If this could last at least a month, I would be so grateful.

Dinner was wonderful. However, I could hardly remember what I ordered. I was thinking about what Dana was really trying to say with just those words, *"That's why I'm falling in love with you." So Dana is falling, not quite there, I guess? Maybe I shouldn't put too much of myself on those words. Maybe I'm over thinking it?*

Later, in the cab and on our way back to the hotel with Dana's arm around me and my head on Dana's shoulder, I whispered, "I accept, I think I'm falling in love with you too." I said it very quietly, just so I could hear my own words.

***

The next morning, Dana was up at five as usual. Dana began to give me a kiss on the forehead. I tilted my head and said, "Don't you dare."

Dana planted a kiss right on my lips. "See you later, honey," I said.

Getting out of bed, I changed from my sexy negligee into my T-shirt and panties. *Oh, so comfortable*, I thought.

My notebook was next to my cell phone. I picked up the cell phone. Looking at its dark face and thought, *Oh God, it's time to return to Earth.*

I pushed the button and waited as it shook and beeped. Then the screen did a dynamic graphic display. I thought, *Is all this necessary just to turn on a cell phone?* Finally, after what seemed minutes, it was on. Voicemail was full. I wasn't even going to look at the messages.

First voicemail was "Okay, Lisa, it's me, give me a call." That was Paula about the time I was leaving Pittsburg.

Then Paula kept calling. "Lisa, call me." Then, "Lisa, where the hell are you? Call me." Then, "Lisa, this isn't funny call me now!" Then, "Lisa, it's Monday; give it up and call me." Then, "Whoever has Lisa hostage, hear me loud and clear, let her go! The FBI is on the case." Then, "Okay, I've called the cops; Lisa is officially a missing person. If you don't return her, I'll hunt you down and kill you. And Lisa, if you just not answering my calls and texts, I'm going to fucking kill you myself! Goddamn it!"

"Oh God, I pissed off my best friend. Shit," I said aloud. *I have been so absorbed in finding myself and being with Dana. I never took the time to call Paula and tell her where I was and what I was doing. Bad girl! Bad, bad girl!* I scolded myself.

It took me five minutes to build up the courage to call her back. I wish I had some scotch around here or even better, tequila.

169

No luck. Just coffee. *Okay, coffee, and sit in my comfy chair.* It was still dark, but the moon was still up. The moon was about half full. Just like my courage, half full.

I hit speed dial. I was still trying to think of a way to cover myself. Captured by pirates came to mind; after all, I was in Pittsburg. *Girl, you're too funny by half,* I was thinking.

Paula answered.

"Yes, I'm okay. No, I'm in Hawaii. No. Yes. No. No. Yes. I just had to get away. What? I don't know, I had to meet someone. Who? Myself, I had to find myself. I was sitting on a beach in Hawaii. No. Yes, I'm serious. Why? Because I had to learn a secret. Okay, okay. Yes, I'm a bitch, a bitch bastard; I'm a fucking bitch slut. What? Yes I'm a fucking bitch shit, got that. Anymore? Okay, I'm a bitch, bitch, bitch shit. Bitch again? Okay. Can I just step in here? Okay. Still with it. Yes, I'm a slut, bitch shit, got it. Now? Okay, I'm just going to break in here. I met somebody! Yes. Yes. Well, yes we did. Dana. Oh God, don't get me started. No. No. I'm not going to tell you. No. No. No, I'm not. Well, maybe when I get home. No. Sunday, I'm going to stop in LA and visit my daughter Bridget and granddaughter Keela. I don't know, I'll text you. No, I can take a cab. No. Yes, I love you. Okay, I'm a bitch." *Well, that went better than I thought.*

With Paula, satisfied, I felt like I could move on to the texts. Are you kidding me, 112 texts!

I skipped through the texts, just reading one here and one there. All of them were about business or flight changes, which reminded me to make new flight reservations. Then a text from my son, Sean, popped up. It was posted on Monday. *How you doing. I think I met a girl. I'll let you know. Love you.*

I immediately texted him back. *Do you mean you met someone who you think is a girl. Ha ha. More details please. Love and miss you.*

A few minutes later, I received my answering text, *It's a girl. Ha ha. Date Friday night. Love you. Miss you too.*

With all the correspondence done, I called and made flight reservations. Then I picked up my notebook. On my page, I wrote, *Long distance relationships.* I thought about that for quite a while then continued, *They don't work,* and then *How to make it work?* Thinking about that, I wrote, *We both have to be on the same page. Okay,* I thought, *we need to write that page.*

Dana had not returned by eleven, so I cleaned up, dressed, and headed for the lobby.

I looked around for Porter; he was standing by the main desk. "Aloha, Porter. How's your day in paradise? "

"Miss Lisa, lovely, and now even more complete seeing you." He was always so nice to everyone.

"Do you know Dana?" I asked.

"But of course. We all know Dana. Quite a person. Dana has been coming here for years." Porter waved around the lobby.

I decided to pry a little bit. "Hummm, have you seen Dana with, you know, anybody else...you know." I stumbled through the question.

"Why, of course. You." Porter smiled.

"You know, besides me," I pressed.

"No, not really. Dana is usually very busy. Usually does the work and leaves," Porter lied "I've never seen Dana take so much free time or look so happy. You are a great influence."

"Well, if you see Dana, I'm at a table by the pool. Thank you, Porter. Aloha." Knowing I'm not going to get anything from him. But I did feel better.

"No problem. Aloha." Porter said, giving me the no problem sign.

***

Dana showed up about an hour later. I had the table set with champagne in an ice bucket, orange juice, fresh fruit, and a basket of pastries.

"Hi, beautiful," Dana called out and leaning over gave me a kiss on the lips. "Sorry, I took so long. Achmed can say ten necessary words but takes about a thousand to do it. It takes a while."

Pouring a mimosa, Dana settled in and said, "What do you want to do today? I'm free."

"I've got some ideas, but first..."

"Does it involve scarves?" Dana broke in hopefully.

"Maybe later. But first, as I was saying...I have to leave tomorrow. Time to get back to Earth," I said.

"Oh. Well, I was going to stay...I mean if you were," Dana said, slightly deflated.

"Really?" I said, thinking that Dana really wanted to be with me.

"Yeah, really. But if you're leaving then. I guess I'll take the tomorrow noon flight back to Atlanta." Dana said kind of down.

"I'm stopping in LA 'til Sunday, to see my daughter and granddaughter. I haven't seen them for such a long time." I said, not really wanting to leave.

"That's nice," Dana said. "I would like to meet them someday."

That's kind of the direction I was going. "Now what," I said, making the claw marks in the air. "Do you call me? Do I call you? Do we trade calls? Or...do you, you know, kind of...you know, forget to call; kind of break it off?" I asked Dana.

"Beautiful," Dana said, "I'll call you lots every day. I don't want to lose you. What about you? Are you going to do the, I forgot to call, break it off thing? That would make me very, very unhappy." He said putting on a pouty face.

"Honey, I want to hold on to you as long as I can. But I've had experience with long distance relationships. Absence makes the heart go wander, I've been told. Not me. Someone else went wandering," I said.

Dana reached over and took my hand. "Beautiful, I'm not going to lose you."

I sat there, looking at Dana thinking, *This is too good to be true. It just can't be real.*

BRIDGET AND I

Chapter 19

The warm, dry, slightly pungent Los Angeles air hit me right in the face as I stepped out the door at baggage claim in LAX.

I stood at the curb with twice as many bags as I had started with from of Pittsburg. Pittsburg seemed such a long time ago, but it was only last Friday, a week ago. *So much can change in a week,* I thought to myself.

The conversation from the night before kept replaying itself in my head.

"Hello, sweetie. Guess what? I'm coming to LA to visit you and Keela." I was so looking forward to seeing my daughter and granddaughter.

"Really? When?" Bridget asked.

"Tomorrow afternoon. I'll text you the flight information," I said excitedly.

"Not really a good time, Lisa," Bridget said flatly.

"Sorry. I'm flying back from Hawaii, and I can't change my flight," I said.

"How long are you going to be here?" She asked.

"I was thinking 'til Sunday. I got to get back to work Monday," I said.

"That won't work. We're going out of town Saturday and Sunday." Rather a strong rejection, I thought.

"Okay, whatever. Just overnight then. I'll leave Saturday morning. Okay?" I said, disappointed.

"Okay, I'll work on something. You might have to stay in a hotel, maybe not. Let me arrange things."

"Okay, if I'm going to be a...," I started.

"No, no; I've got to go. See you at the curb. Love you." I didn't quite believe her.

"Love you too, sweetie." I said as the phone went dead.

***

Bridget had found a place at the curb, about 150 feet from where I was standing, about ten minutes after I came out of baggage claim. LAX was such a pain. She popped the trunk as I approached. I stuffed my two bags and briefcase in the trunk. The big Hawaiian straw bag with the presents I had bought for them in Hawaii was dropped in the backseat.

I slid into the front seat. Bridget cleared her throat. "How was the flight?"

"It went up, it stayed up, and it came down as planned. Couldn't be better," I answered. Looking around, I asked, "Where is Keela?"

"Keela is with Ashley!" Ashley was my first ex.

"So, when do I get to see her?" I asked, a little put out.

"Sorry, Lisa. Ashley took Keela to Disneyland. They are staying overnight at the new hotel. They won't be back 'til tomorrow. Then we are leaving for Tahoe for a few days. Tahoe has been arranged for a few weeks. We're going with Debra, Mark, Chuck, and their boy, so we can't change it."

"Why didn't you tell me Keela wasn't going to be here yesterday?" Now I was getting really pissed.

"Ashley didn't tell us they were going 'til last night. Keela really wanted to go to Disneyland," Bridget said coolly.

Now I was really pissed. "Oh, I get it." I wanted to scream. Bridget, knowing me, was bracing herself for what might come out of my mouth next. But I just sat quietly in my seat. I reached into my purse and just touched my notebook. I thought about all that I have learned in the past week. It was the time to put some of that into action, accept or reject or change the conditions.

"You know I wanted to see Keela, at least for a little bit," I quietly said.

"Look, Lisa. I'm just trying to keep peace in the family," she said very loudly. "You're never here, so...whatever." Her voice trailed off. "Whatever."

My mind had filled up with several responses to her tirade: a dry "Not doing a very good job are you?" A cold "So when did Ashley become your best friend?" Or playing the wounded parent, "So, I mean that little to you? I should not have come. I probably should never come. I mean you just want me out of your life. Don't you?" Perhaps with a demand to turn around and then throw their presents on the ground as I get out of the car.

I was inclined to go with the wounded parent, but we both just sat their quietly. *So I have to accept that I'm not going to see Keela because of my ex.* Because my ex wanted to hurt me and because Bridget went along with it.

Okay. What would I write down? I can't do that now. I've got to use what I've learned.

I have to reject getting mad at my daughter. I know I'm not easy to love. God, what does Dana see in me? I know I'm not here enough. I know I wasn't in Bridget's life enough, even when she was young. I know she resented me during the divorce and after. I know Ashley exerted as much influence as possible, and from my experience, she can be very devious. Ashley changes the perceptions of the past to fix an agenda, one that would specifically benefit Ashley or put me down. So all that was left was to change the conditions.

After several miles, I said, taking a deep breath, "You know I love you and Keela more than anything. Right?"

"I know. We love you too" came an automatic reply.

"Is Scott." My son in law "Going to join us tonight for dinner?"

"No, he's working on a case. He won't be home 'til after dinner."

How usual, I thought. *My own family doing everything they can to avoid me. That's been going on for a long time. But to be fair, I'm never here, and Ashley lives nearby. In fact, most of my family lives in California. I don't, and I don't have much choice in that right now. Maybe if I had lived close by, they would have accepted me. Maybe.*

Now comes changing the conditions, I thought. "Would you like to go shopping with me?"

"What?" That was not what she was expecting. "What? Shopping for what?"

"I don't know, just shopping. We haven't done that in years, decades. You know, spend the afternoon together, just you and me, shopping. Please. Please. I would love to spend some time just with my daughter. Please?" I begged.

Bridget looked over at me, thought for more than a minute. I sat quietly, waiting for her decision. *Accept or reject. I had to accept her decision whatever it was.*

"Well, okay. Just for a little while," she finally said.

"Cool." I was all smiles. "Can we go to Nordstrom, please?"

"Okay, there is one just a little out of the way. Not that far from here." She had a little smile for the first time that day.

"Very cool," I said.

"Why specifically Nordstrom?" She asked.

"The gods of Nordstrom, have been very good to me lately."

As we turned to into the shopping center, she asked, "You'll explain that to me someday, right?"

"It has to do with a scarlet cocktail dress and matching shoes. Long story," I said.

"Figures, it had to have something to do with dresses," she said matter-of-factly.

The gods of Nordstrom were indeed good to me again. My daughter and I shopped for four hours.

We tried on clothes. We found clothing for each other and ourselves. Lots of "Do you think this is too tight around here?" And, "Really, Lisa that's way too short," or "Does this make my butt look big?" Quickly followed by, "Honey you have no butt."

We tried on shoes. They all looked great. Bridget tried to get me to buy some flats. That fell flat.

We browsed the counters, getting makeovers at the makeup counter and spraying perfume on our arms. We tried on big expensive sunglasses, made faces at each other, and laughed a lot. We left Nordstrom loaded down with bags in both hands.

After we loaded ourselves into the car, filling the trunk and most of the backseat, Bridget turned to me. "How about going to dinner?"

"I would love to, as long as it's not some hoity-toity place," I said.

Bridget looked at me a little puzzled. "What's hoity-toity?"

"It's an inside joke," I answered with a wave of the hand "Any place you like, any place you pick, I'll love."

Bridget picked a restaurant on the side of a hill overlooking the Pacific Ocean.

"The view is just as beautiful from this side of the ocean as it is from the other side," I noted out loud as we took out seats at the table.

"Lisa, you seem, I don't know, more relaxed. More tuned in, less self-absorbed. I don't know, more understanding." She said, "I enjoyed today."

"I don't know if I'm less self-adsorbed, but I do have a fresh perspective on life." I continued, "And this was one of the best days in my life. Thank you."

She let that sink in. "So why did you go to Hawaii? Business?"

"Secret mission," I answered.

"What?" She said, puzzled.

"It's a little complicated to explain." I took a deep breath and a sip of wine. "I went to find myself, and I did. I found myself sitting by the ocean in the sand, at about four in the morning, a little drunk."

"I bet," she replied.

"Anyway, after talking to myself for quite a while. Myself told me the secret. And I've been working on it ever since," I explained.

"Well, what is the secret?" She asked

"Everybody wants to know what the secret is, but if I tell everyone, it won't be a secret anymore," I said seriously and then smiled. "It seen so obvious to me now. You have probably know it all along. I'm just getting to understand it."

"Well, what is it?" She pressed, interested.

"I'm responsible for my own happiness," I said, a little proud of myself.

"Is that it? You're responsible for your own happiness. That's it?" She asked, incredulously. "Seems kind of obvious to me."

"I told you it was obvious. Your way ahead of me in these things, daughter."

We sat studying our menus, sipping our wine.

"It's not really that easy you know. Lots of messy parts," I offered.

She went back to her menu. The waiter came by, and we ordered our meal. She sat quietly, studying my face. After a few minutes, she finally leaned forward. "I don't really understand you, you know? I didn't get a chance to understand you. You were never around."

"I know. Part of the paths we take in life, sometimes we know what we're doing, sometimes we don't. We all just have to live with it," I answered as best I could.

"Don't, don't try and explain yourself to me now," she said, showing the temper I gave her.

"I won't. How's Scott doing?" I asked, trying to change the subject. Bridget sat in silence. The mood had turn and not in my favor.

I thought it best to just wait it out. See how she was going to react. Eventually and reluctantly she answered, "He's doing fine. Works a lot. We do as much as we can with Keela."

"And Keela, what's she up to?" Bridget went on to tell me a bit about what was happening in their lives. Places they are going, parties they have or are going to. Nothing about Ashley or Jessie my two exes.

Both exes lived in Southern California. In fact, most of my extended family lived in California. I thought of Jessie, my second and favorite ex. Ashley lived closer to Bridget and is one of her natural parents. Even Bridget understood that Ashley was more possessive, controlling, difficult, and demanding. Ashley, during our marriage and several marriages thereafter, had been a serial cheater. And because I was the one asking for the divorce, Ashley had it out for me. So any chance Ashley got, Ashley tried to belittle, hurt, or embarrass me. That's why Keela was at Disneyland; that was Ashley's way of saying, "I'm in charge here."

As Bridget talked, she began to lighten up, became more herself. I asked her what projects she was into, and I listened with deep interest and only a few comments for the rest of the meal.

Looking at her, I could not help but smile and think what a beautiful and intelligent woman she had become.

As the sun grew in size and lost some of its brightness, the sun slipped out of this world and into the next. Bridget smiled and said, "I had a wonderful day. Really, I did."

"Thank you, so did I. A wonderful, wonderful day" I said as I reached out to squeeze her hand.

As we were walking to the car, she stopped and looked at me. "I don't know what happened to you in Hawaii. You have changed, and you are positively glowing. You look beautiful."

I smiled deeply and unsuccessfully held back tears as I hugged her and said, "Thank you."

HOME

Chapter 20

The next morning, I was dressed and ready to go early. We stopped at Starbucks for coffee to go.

At LAX, as I was unloading my bags, Bridget came around the car to give me a hug and a kiss.

"Be sure and let me know how Keela likes her gift," I asked.

"Sure. I love you and have a safe flight," she said. That time, I believed her.

***

Paula was waiting at the curb at ORD, Chicago's O'Hare airport, her trunk was already open. Paula was arguing with the parking cop. As I wheeled my baggage cart out the door, I could hear her say, "See, there she is now. So can we load up and get going?" As she threw her hands up in the air in a frustrated gesture. The man in blue walked away, shaking his head.

"It took you long enough," Paula said as she wrapped her arms around me, and I hugged her back. We shared a quick kiss on the lips, and we loaded up.

"What was that?" I asked, gesturing toward the traffic cop.

"Dumbass wanted me to go around. I argued with him for ten minutes 'til you finally got your ass here."

"Didn't he give you a ticket?" I asked.

"Hell no. I took his pen."

"What?"

"What's he going to do? He didn't have a gun or even handcuffs. Just a stupid ticket book, and look...no pen," she said as she held up a pen.

As we drove away, I saw a police car pull up in the spot we had just left.

"Did he have a radio?" I asked.

"Yea, I guess," she answered.

"You're incredible," I said as we left the airport terminal.

"Yeah, I know," she said with a little smile.

"So, a little vacation in Hawaii without telling me, or taking me...bitch."

"We both can't be gone. The business would fall apart," I argued. "I'm always here. I never get to go anywhere. You're the one pulling all the strings."

Paula ran the place. She had a way with the employees that I didn't have. Nobody tried to bully her or fib to her. She was in control. Everyone said "yes, ma'am" from the 89-pound Asian girl putting parts together the size of a fingernail, assembled to the 350-pound forklift-truck loader guy. For all of her five-foot-two inch, 105-pounds, she was the mightiest woman or man on the floor.

"Okay, what's this secret? You are going to tell me. Right?"

"Oh dear. I need wine if I'm going to go into all that again," I uttered.

"Regular Saturday place?" She asked.

"Sure...I missed it," I said.

"What? You didn't go hungry in Hawaii, did you?"

"No. Now what's this about the Rayman account?" Turning the subject to business so that we could get off my trip to Hawaii for a little bit.

***

We settled in at our end of the bar in our regular chairs. The Arrow was our place, particularly on Saturdays. The bartenders all knew us by name and what we drank. But Eric had become our favorite bartender. So when he saw us coming across the street, he had our regular glasses of wine sitting in our places by the time we sat down.

After the typical "How have you been? Where have you been?" and "Would you believe she went to Hawaii and didn't even tell me or even call me. *And* the bitch did even take her phone messages." Taking a breath and pausing to look at me she said "Bitch, B-I-T-C-H." and then hugged me and kissed me. Eric smiled and wiped a clean wine glass over and over again.

"Are you ever going to forgive me?" I asked.

"No" was her quick answer. We settled in and continued with some small talk with Eric.

"Okay…What's this secret?" She asked.

I took a sip of my wine and started in. "That I'm responsible for my own happiness and…"

"Duh! No shit! Now tell me about this Dana," she demanded.

"Humm…" I paused for effect. "Dana is the most wonderful person you'll ever meet. Dana is tall, blonde, blue eyed, and very athletic."

"So you did it! How was it?" She said loudly.

"Shut up! Or at least lower you voice." I admonished, knowing I could never actually shut her up.

In a deeper, but not quieter, voice, she asked, "So you did it! How was it?" She crossed her arms on the bar and leaned toward me. "Tell me everything. From the beginning. Don't leave anything out."

Before I could begin, her cell phone rang.

"Hi, honey." She mouthed that it was Dave.

Paula and Dave were the best fit I ever saw. Paul always said, "You got to keep picking the fruit until you find the sweet one," and she should know after three marriages.

"No, I just picked her up. Yes, we're at the Arrow. Don't you dare. We've got a lot of catching up to do." Paula went on, "Love you. See you tonight, don't wait up."

Setting down her cell phone, she looked at me. "Well?"

"Well, when I left Pittsburg, I stayed up all the way to Hawaii.

I sat on the beach 'til dawn, meeting myself, and drinking wine."

"Not that part! Tell me about Dana?" She urged, waving me on.

I gave her the "like really" look. "The next evening, or was it the same evening?"

"Whatever." She waved me on again.

I gave her the "like really" look again. "I was hungry and wanted a drink."

"So...?" She tried to move me along again.

"So I went to the bar. I had a gin martini and a basket of chicken wings. I had wing sauce all across my face, my cheek, my forehead, and on my white blouse, and then this fresh martini showed up."

"You didn't order it, right?" She filled in.

"No, I didn't. In fact, I tried to give it back."

"Really, you tried to give back a free drink?" She laughed.

"Really. The bartender wouldn't let me and pointed out this blonde on the far side of the bar. I told the bartender to thank the blonde. I downed the martini and left. I didn't say thank you or anything. Just got out of there."

"You accepted a cocktail, didn't say thank you, and ran out. That's how you get someone interested in you?" She asked, incredulous.

"I guess Dana likes messy women."

"You're all that and a bag of chips." It was Paula's favorite saying. "Go on," she demanded.

I did, leaving out some of the juicier parts, even when Paula demanded more detail.

As we talked, we ordered appetizers and shared them. After awhile, the conversation drifted off in different directions. Paula finally asked, "So where is this notebook?"

"Right here." I said, patting my purse.

"Let me see." She reached out.

"No, it's private, like a diary," I said.

"Come on. We don't have any secrets," she coaxed.

"No." I was steadfast. "It's what I think about people and how...well, what they did and what I did. No."

"Okay," She was dejected. "How about just the parts about me? Please."

There was no getting out of it until I gave in a little. "Well, just some of it." I took out my notebook. I flipped to the page headed Paula.

"Wow, a whole page just for me?" Paula sounded amazed.

"No. Three pages." I thumbed the pages. I had never shared my notebook with anyone, not even Dana. It was messier than I thought. I should have never told her about the notebook.

As I scanned down the page, shaking my head, looking for something to share, it was then that I realized what a positive influence Paula had been in my life.

"Come on. Give." She was always trying to get me to get to the point.

"Okay. Here are some of the nicer things you said to me." And I listed them.

"Thank you. Now how about some of the bad things," she demanded.

"No much, not nearly as much as Ashley. Not much at all." I closed the notebook.

"You probably have an entire chapter devoted to the nasty things that bitch Ashley did to you." She waited a moment. "Now me."

"Oh really, you don't..." Seeing the look on her face, I knew I had gone too far, and now I had to tell her at least something.

"Okay, but I'm over it. I was just getting perspective." I opened the notebook to the page that had some of the hurtful things Paula had said to me. Most of it she didn't even know had hurt me.

A few things were read off then she looked up. "I'm sorry," she said and threw her arms around me giving me a big hug.

"It's all gone, way gone," I said. "And I love you. You're my best and closest friend, closer than family."

"I love you so much," she said, and we both reached for our wine glasses and toasted each other. "BFFs forever," we both said.

After a few minutes, I said, "I think I'll call Dana." and dialed his number, only to get his voicemail. Disappointed, I tried to put some of the things I knew about Dana out of my mind. *There are good reasons Dana didn't answer my call,* I thought. *There has to be.*

We had about reached our wine limit. "I'm so glad to be home," I said.

"Me too. Now it's time to take you to your home." She pulled out her credit card and called Eric over.

***

The house was waiting patiently for me. The maid service had done their job; there was no dust and the plants were watered, and the house was at the right temperature.

I went up to my bedroom, leaving my heels in the entry and only taking one bag with me. I undressed and took a quick shower, shedding the travel odors and dust. I put on my panties and T-shirt. *So comfortable.* I started downstairs when I heard my cell phone ring, and I ran the rest of the way down to the entry and fished through my purse for my cell phone. "Hi, beautiful. How's LA?" Dana asked.

"I'm in Chicago. Just got in the house a little bit ago as a matter of fact," I said, a bit out of breath.

"I thought you were going to be in LA until tomorrow? What happened?" Dana asked.

"Ashley, my ex, and bad timing." I pouted.

"Sorry. What did Ashley do?" Dana was concerned.

"Just what I should have expected Ashley to do. I'm over it. In fact, Bridget and I had a wonderful time. I think it was good for us to have some girl time." I followed up with, "Are you home?"

"Not yet. I just got off the airplane." *No wonder Dana didn't answer my earlier call. And I was all nervous Dana was ignoring me.* "I thought you were flying home yesterday?" I asked, a little suspicious.

"Complications with shipping. I had to spend an extra day," Dana explained.

"How are we ever going to get together when we're always off schedule?" I questioned.

"Well, now that you brought that up, are you going to be home Thursday through Sunday?"

"Yeah, I guess," I said. "Why?"

"Because I had Alyssa make some calls. I got an appointment at Water Tower Place Friday morning."

"Really? Great. I already miss you. When are you coming in?" I asked excitedly.

"Thursday, about six-thirty," Dana said.

"Oh great. I'll pick you up. I can't wait," I said.

We chatted for a bit as I made my way into the living room and my comfy chair.

"That appointment Friday," I asked, "can you make it in the afternoon?"

"Yes, probably. Why?"

"I want to take you to work and show you off. Then I have some ideas for Friday evening downtown," I explained.

The world was right again. I was home, tired, happy, and still couldn't sleep.

***

Sunday morning, I called Paula as soon as I had my first cup of coffee.

"Guess what? Guess who's coming to town." I didn't wait. "Dana!"

"When? Super. When?"

"Thursday. This Thursday, four days from now."

"Great! We'll pick Dana up," Paula started.

"We'll? No, just me. I want Dana all to myself," I said.

"No way, kiddo. We pick Dana up. You introduce us, then Dana and I kiss. Perhaps a little foreplay, then we meet Dave for dinner. Done!" Paula laid out her plans.

That was one of those arguments that, once again, I was not going to win.

On Thursday, at six-fifteen, we parked at the curb, popped the trunk, and waited on the sidewalk for Dana to appear. The parking cop was walking the line, making the cars go around. Seeing him, Paula waved. "Hi, sweetie. Remember me?"

The parking cop looked up, shook his head, and kept walking right by us.

"Kind of rude...don't you think?" Paula said. "Seriously." Then she turned away for the parking cop's direction and broke out laughing.

We both were still laughing when Dana exited the terminal, bags in tow. As promised, Paula ran up to Dana and laid one right on the lips, much to Dana's surprise.

The ride to the Arrow was mostly Paula pumping Dana for information. The line of questioning was only broken up by Paula telling embarrassing stories about me.

"Paula, shut up" became the most frequent words out of my mouth followed by "Oh God," as I hid my face under my hand to cover the blushing.

Dave had commandeered our corner of the bar. With his Absolut vodka drink in hand, Dave stood and gave Dana a hug then mentioned, "You might want to wipe Paula's lipstick off your lips," with a laugh.

Eric gave us a warm welcome. True to form, Paula's wine was already next to Dave's seat and mine sitting next to Paula's seat. "So, Dana, I've heard so much about you, but I never heard what you drank?" Eric never let anyone go dry.

"Rainbow martini, please." Dana didn't expect Eric to know that drink.

"Lemon or lime?" Eric shot back.

Dana was surprised, but only a few seconds passed before Dana answered, "Lime."

Eric hung at our corner of the bar. Dave, Paula, and Eric all but interrogated Dana. Nicely interrogated, no water-boarding. I tried to intercede, but I was either brushed off by Paula, or Dana would touch my arm and go ahead and spill the beans. Everyone seemed to delight in making me blush.

Several appetizers were ordered and shared. No one wanted to interrupt the conversation with something so common as dinner. Eric, as usual, kept all our drinks fresh.

Two and a half hours later, wanting Dana to myself, I made the excuse that Dana must be tired from the flight. It still took fifteen minutes to wrap things up and give each other hugs and kisses.

On the way out, Eric give me the thumbs up.

***

On Friday, I dressed in a different short red sheath dress, matching red pumps, and a business jacket. It was very businesslike, but when the jacket came off, the outfit turned into a sexy evening outfit. We visited the plant and made the tour, made nice, and greeted everyone. It was Friday; Paula is a very good manager. Some employees don't want to come to work on Fridays or Mondays. She checked the stats. Friday was free lunch day; today, it was pizza. Monday morning was coffee, tea, and sometime donuts, sometime sandwiches from McDonald's. But it's all put away at eight forty-five. If you are not there by then, you don't get anything except for me.

Something always ends up on my desk.

Did I tell you I'm habitually late for work? Well, not work but getting to the plant. Work starts almost as soon as I wake up, checking and answering e-mails then I do my physical exercises. Finally, I dress as the CEO for a nice-sized business. I'm always in the office by ten or before. Well, a little before.

We were out of the plant by 2:00 p.m. That wasn't easy with Paula trying to find reasons to delay our exit. It was two thirty by the time we reached Water Tower Place.

"So you go do your deal, I'll go shopping. Call me when you're done," I said as I walked into Water Tower Place.

"Ah, so what is it we're going to do after?" Dana asked.

"You'll see," I said as I began to walk away.

"What are going to go do?" Dana called after me.

"I told you, shopping." I turned around. "For panties," I said over my shoulder.

It took Dana several hours to do the deal. We met in Victoria's Secret. I made Dana uncomfortable, showing my purchases. It wasn't so much the purchases but how I show Dana my new sexy purchases. We took the glass elevator down to the upper lobby and the escalator, down to the main lobby. Just a quick trip across the street to the Hancock Building. We made our way to the north side doors to the elevator taking us directly to the ninety-sixth floor bar. In a few minutes, we had secured two seats by the window, we were looking out west over the city, directly into the sunset. We settled into our seats and ordered our cocktails.

The sun seemed to kick up red dust off the prairie, which attached itself to the undersides of the few clouds in the sky as well as the jet contrails crisscrossing the skies over O'Hare airport. Then as the sun ducked below the perfectly flat horizon, the city lights well below our feet were slowly taking over the night. By the time the sun grabbed the last red rays from the sky, Chicago's lighting had taken over. Streaks of yellow light led like cat scratches off into the distance. It didn't take much to think of those yellow lit streets as yellow brick roads.

After a while and some small talk I turned to Dana and in my serious voice said. "Dana, serious now."

"Okay, I know that voice. Serious."

"I'm going to Phoenix next Sunday, for a week."

Dana sat for a moment, maybe a little longer. "I know of some good western artists in Phoenix. I always wanted to visit them. Maybe do some business. Next week would be good."

I squeezed Dana's hand. "Honey, you don't have to do that... You don't have to follow me around, taking care of me."

"I'm not following you around only because you're beautiful. You're also good for business. You should see the deal I made today," Dana said excitedly.

"If you're sure. You don't have to," I pressed.

"Just try and keep me away." Dana leaned forward and gave me a light kiss on the lips.

PHOENIX

Chapter 21

"No, Paula, you're not walking me in. Done," I said as we parked the car on the upper level at O'Hare airport. "I'm a big girl now."

Dave popped the trunk, and both Dave and Paula got out to help me with my single bag.

Dave hugged me and whispered in my ear, "See you next week." Paula squeezed me and buried her head in my cleavage and, through tears, said only, "Love you."

I was doing all right up to then. For the three hours at my house, Paula, checked and rechecked my suitcase. Then she answered every phone call: "It's Sean, here," "It's Bridget, here," "It's Dana, here," "It's work, I'll take that." Then she asked the same question over and over again: "You sure she's the right doctor?," "Why Phoenix?" and "Why can't I go with you?" She always got the same answers. "Yes," "Because...," and "Who's going to watch the business?" Now standing at the curb, holding each other, I said through my own tears, "Love you."

I started toward the terminal, turned and gave her the hand sign that commanded "Stay."

***

It had been a dreadful few days since Dana left. Rain would have been a relief. It just drizzled, gray, cold, and always wet. It just drizzled. "Heavenly skies, just spit it out and get it over with," I begged.

I sat next to the window, watching the drizzle slid down the side of the airplane. The rain made little streams of water down my oval window. It just couldn't get any more depressing than this. The only bright spot, I held in my heart. Yesterday, I happily gave up trying to talk Dana out of going to Phoenix. Dana would be there for me.

Somewhere over Nebraska, my well-worn notebook found its way into my lap. I read, *I am responsible for my own happiness.* Then it took me half a state to write down, *I am responsible for my own life, I need to do this thing.* I knew that before I wrote it down; still, I wondered.

***

Dana had arrived earlier, rented a car, and booked us into the hotel next to the hospital.

"No. Don't meet me at baggage claim, that's just plain...ahhh, not necessary." I caught myself before saying "stupid." Then my female rationale kicked in. "Please, meet me at the curb. That way, I wouldn't have to walk very far."

As I exited baggage claim, I found Dana leaning up against the rental car, arms crossed. "Hi, beautiful. Need a ride?"

I crossed the service traffic lane and into Dana's arms and cried. "It's alright, beautiful. I'm here," Dana said petting my hair, repeating it over and over 'til I backed off and dried my tears with the back of my hand, both of my hands.

In the car on the way to the hotel, I sat quietly gazing out the passenger window, seeing nothing. *How did I lose my strength?* I wondered. *All these years, all those operations, and now I break down at the end. I used to be strong. I did it all myself. I was strong then. I used to be strong.*

Dana reached over and took my hand, holding it. I was limp. Maybe it was the drugs the doctor gave me with instructions to take them before the airplane left O'Hare. More pills to take when I landed, and still more pills to take before I went to bed. By the time I had reached Phoenix, my body and spirit felt limp.

Dana guided a limp and slightly drugged woman through the hotel, up to our room. As we entered the room, everything came crashing down around my head. Dana was just so good, and I was just so dirty. I pushed away from Dana. "I got to shower."

***

The shower was hot and long. Naked, I examined myself in the mirror. *What does Dana see in me? I am so not beautiful. I am so afraid. I used to be strong.*

I put on my T-shirt and panties, hair wet and no makeup. Just plain, bare me. I exited the bathroom, looking for Dana.

Dana had arranged for a room facing east into the sunrise. It had a balcony. Somehow, Dana had gotten a small love seat placed on the balcony where he was seated in the warm Phoenix night air, quietly gazing off into the darkening night. Quietly, I sat beside Dana and his arm slipped around me, pulling me into warmth and love.

"I don't know why you love me. I'm such a mess." I began to sob.

"I guess I just love messy women," Dana said as I settled deeper into that warmth, and as the last series of pills kicked in and I began to fall asleep. Then I understood. I didn't have to be the strong one this time.

***

The next morning before sunrise, wearing only a paper gown, the nurses began to push needles into my veins, and stuck electrical sensors in familiar and strange places. The new set of drugs were doing their job, as was Dana, who calmly held my hand. Nothing was as it should be. I wasn't strong. I wasn't weak. I wasn't afraid. I wasn't awake. I wasn't asleep. Dana's words landed softly on ears, but held no meaning. Eventually, Dana was directed out of the room, and before leaving, lightly kissed my lips. "See you soon, beautiful." Something in me felt Dana go. I could not raise my voice. "Stay," I wanted to say. I could not even raise my hand.

I was rolled into the operating room, and another bottle was hooked up to one of the needles in my arm. As the valve was turned, allowing fluid into my veins I heard, "Hi, sweetie. You're going to sleep now." It was the last thing I remembered.

***

A new life later, I had tubes in my nose, mouth, and arms and wires attached to various parts of my body. Then someone unceremoniously pried my left eyelid open with their thumb. "Thank, God, finally." They were the first words I heard, followed by "Get Dr. Meyer."

Something had not gone quite right. Instead of the four or five hours I was expected to be out, I was well into the fifth day before they let me come to. I was not feeling good. I wanted to throw up. In fact, I did after they pulled the tubes out of my throat. It was just clear liquid, leftover water from the tubes. As the nurse cleaned me up, the next words I remember were, "That's normal, honey. You'll be fine now."

Dr. Meyer entered the room and did an evaluation of my condition. "You're going to be okay, honey," he said before squeezing my hand. Looking down at me he said, "Dana's outside. I just want to check a few things before I let her in, okay?"

A few minutes later, Dana was allowed into the room. "Hi, beautiful! You're back." She planted a kiss on my dry, chapped lips, knowing better than to kiss me on the forehead.

Identity

"Honey, you're still here," I croaked through half open and drugged eyes.

"Yes, and I've got your key," Dana said, holding up the hotel key card.

"Oh God, I love you so much!" Was all I could think to say. He had remembered me holding up the card that night in Hawaii. It was a symbol of my acceptance.

***

One week became two. The second week, I was allowed to stay in our hotel room with my own hospital-issued wheelchair. I sat on the balcony every morning, waiting for mother sun to come to me, letting her powers heal me, and the power of her touch brought life back into my body. I slowly began to bloom.

By the second day of the second week, Dana was becoming antsy. I still wasn't allowed wine, and I didn't want it near me. It was just too tempting. It didn't take much to get Dana to go see the Phoenix artists. "No, I'm not leaving this room. Go do something useful," I would command. Later it became "No, you go have dinner with them. I'm not leaving this room. Besides, I didn't bring any shoes that go with this wheelchair." I tried to joke, a lame joke. I mostly sat on the balcony. I mostly slept. I mostly waited for Dana.

My kids and Dana talked every day I was in the hospital. In the hotel, Dana answered the phone and, if it wasn't work, handed the cell phone over to me if I was awake.

My daily exam at the hospital was showing results. I was gaining strength. I credited Dana and the sun. Both were in my life every morning and every evening. Both gave me strength.

Finally, I was ordered to give back the wheel chair and go home! Dr. Meyer gave us our instructions. "Here's what you have to do." He said. "Lots of rest and no sex for two more weeks.

You'll have to take these pills every day for the rest of your life."
Dr. Meyer instructed as she wrote a prescription down in her little
electronic notepad.

"Great." Dana said, "See you in two weeks, babe," he said and
stood up then he paused and laughed and giving me a hand up.

We walked back to the hotel hand in hand. I caught my
reflection on the hotel glass entry door. "Oh God! I am horrible!"
I said. "You've been living with an animal for over a week! A
whiny, miserable animal! I've got to make this up to you. Please,
can I make this up to you?" I begged, turning to Dana.

"Does it involve ropes?" Dana asked laughed hopefully.

"Anything you want, except...you know. First I need to get
beautiful again. Maybe the porter knows of a salon."

"Ain't no Porter here. But I'll ask at the desk," Dana said.

I had packed the scarlet satin dress and heels from Hawaii.
I had my nails colored to match my dress. By that time, I had
bought a perfect clutch, satin red with a red lace covering. By God,
I was going all out tonight.

In the hospital, by design, everyone expects it to be all about
you. You are the center of attention. Everyone asks how you're
feeling. "Super. That's why I'm here in the hospital. Ha ha. I would
laugh but it hurts." I would try to joke away my fear.

From the time I was let out of the hospital and Dana took over
at the hotel, I was not just messy, I was one hot screwed-up mess. At
least in the hospital, after I came to, the nurses had to deal with me.
Now sitting in the salon, bits and pieces came back to me. I really
screwed up. I thought Dana was not calling me beautiful that much
anymore. Well, I wasn't beautiful. And the more I thought about
how I acted, the worse it got, at least in my imagination.

"Hoity-toity?" Dana asked as I was let off at the salon.

"Hoity-toity for sure!" I answered.

The restaurant was done in western-modern. It was situated on a hill, with big windows over-looking Phoenix in the valley. The city's evening lights were only challenged by the desert star lit night sky.

"Mimosa?" Dana asked.

"No." I said, with a smile. "You're so nice to remember that, and just now when I needed you so much."

"Rainbow martini perhaps or mellow melon?" Again, Dana smiled.

"Honey, you got me. Anything you want, almost, and after the next two weeks…anything. Besides, I don't think I should. How about a nice red wine? Red wine's good for you. Right? But I know you want a rainbow martini, or at least see if they know what it is," I said.

The wine was served, the meal ordered. "Okay, seriously now, and honest."

"That voice again. Okay, serious and honest." Dana complied.

"Pinkie promise." I said, offering my pinkie.

"You're really going to do this?" Dana asked, taking my pinkie.

"Did I screw us up? Am I too needy? Was I too needy? Did I whine a lot? Please tell me what I did wrong, and how can I make it up." I tried to plead my case.

"Beautiful, you screwed up. You did almost everything wrong. You kind of pissed me off several times. To tell the truth. Always honest you know…, sometimes…I wasn't with an artist."

That last one dug into me; my breath froze in place. *Was it another girl? Was Dana regretting the old, sick bitch he hooked up with and went back to the younger ones?*

201

"Sometimes, I went to the art museum just so I didn't have to deal with you for a few hours. And sometimes, I would stop at the bar and down a couple of martinis. And sometimes, I would combine the two. And all the time, I worried about you. Never gave up hope when they told me that..." A short pause. "Really, you were not that bad, you were not a bitch, you were not screwing up things between us, and you were most defiantly not sweetness and light. And I'm still deeply in love with you."

Just how is it that when given 120 words, most very nice, that I focus in on just nine words? "Oh thank you. Not being sweetness and light is the part I totally get and believe. I am so sorry about being a pain. So sorry. So sorry. Please forgive me?"

"Yes, of course I forgive you. But you weren't just a pain, you were a frigid pain in the ass with a twelve-inch super fatty mounted on the end of a log splitter." Dana let it hang in the air as I said my mea culpa as fast as I could. "Naaw, you weren't that bad. I'm just trying to get points here."

"Well, you can't get any more points here. You won the game." After a bit I said. "You said, and I quote 'You never gave up hope when they told you that' something. What was that?"

"I'm not supposed to tell." Dana told the truth.

"Who told you that?" I demanded.

"The doctors. So there!" Was the reply.

"Please I need to know. Please," I begged.

"Only that it was touch and go there for a little while. They decided to keep you under. They induced a coma, I think they said so that the drugs and some other little surgeries could work." Dana held my hand. "But it all worked, and you're back with me." I took Dana's hand and placed it on my thigh for comfort.

"OK," I said as I let it settle in to my mind. Then I thought, *I'm going to have to pump Dr. Meyer later.*

The next morning, Dana dropped me at the airport and called for a wheelchair. I objected but Dana insisted. Dana accompanied me to the gate and gave me a kiss as I boarded the flight.

***

At O'Hare, Paula met me at the gate with a wheelchair. "Come on, girl," I complained.

"Orders from Dana," Paula said.

Bill was at the curb, chatting nicely with our parking cop. Bill somehow made friends with everyone. The traffic cop gave me a wave as he walked away to move other cars on, not ours. Paula handed over the wheelchair to the porter. Dave gave me a hug and whispered, "You're late. I expected you more than a week ago."

The next weekend, Dana came up in Chicago for a week! I was feeling better by the following week, so I joined Dana down in Atlanta.

Alyssa was a carbon duplicate of Dana but with much longer blonde hair. She had blue eyes and was tall and dancer thin.

On meeting for the first time at the Atlanta airport, Alyssa threw her arms around me and gave me a kiss on the cheek. Dana had a difficult time getting a word in edgewise as Alyssa and I bonded.

"Dana never stops talking about you." She later told me, "I'm so happy Dana found someone. Ever since Casey, who left when I was four years old. Dana has been in nothing but bad short term relationships."

"What about Casey?" I asked, curious about the other parent. "Oh, nothing," Alyssa answered. "I might get a birthday card every few years. That's about it."

"But." She said changing the subject. "Would you believe that Dana did not date until I was old enough to date? I milked that one. I went on my first date to the junior senior prom at fourteen."

"To tell the truth, when Dana first told me about you, I thought, 'Oh, another chickadee.' Do you know Dana calls you beautiful, like it's your first name? Beautiful Lisa. Anyway, so of course, when Dana first told me about you, I thought you were one of Dana's twenty-year-old brainless babes. But you're older than I. Unusual but a definite plus." Alyssa chatted on like a champion speed-talker. "And you're smart, successful and, I agree, beautiful. How old are you, by the way?"

"Let's leave it at I've got a son ten years older than you. Okay?"

"Really, is he married? Just kidding," Alyssa said.

"No. Just unreliable," I kidded.

"Just between us, girls, how did you get Dana interested in you? Hell, fallen in love with you." Alyssa pressed.

"I really don't know. I guess Dana just loves messy women."

"That's from me." She laughed. "Whatever the mess was, was always spread all over, me, the couch, table, floor, anything near me." For the next six months, Dana and I found reasons to be together not only in Chicago and Atlanta but also New York, Miami, Dallas, just about anywhere east of the Rockies.

When I was in Atlanta, the three of us were almost always together. Alyssa had her own place within walking distance of Dana's place. The formal "appointment only" studio was only a twenty-minute walk from both Dana's and Alyssa's homes.

Alyssa admitted that she was afraid of following Dana's example. Alyssa had only two serious relationships. Both lasted about two and a half years. Both ended with Alyssa throwing their cheating asses to the curb.

Dana and Alyssa had the close relationship that I always wish I had with my kids. I envied that. With almost no effort, the three of us became a family unit.

Identity

I felt that for the first time in a long time that I belonged.

My notebook had found a home in my purse. The first month after the operation, I almost never took it out, and I never wrote in it. I had found my way for a time.

Chapter 22

I had been avoiding the West Coast for the last six months, partly because I wanted to spend my free time with Dana and, when possible, Alyssa. But the bigger part was because I wasn't sure how the family would take to Dana. I thought Bridget would be okay, but I wasn't even sure of that. After all, I knew I was the strange one in the family, and living two thousand miles away didn't help. So what would they think of my new lover?

But Thanksgiving was coming. Often, it was the only time all year I would visit LA. I was expected to show up, if only because they need someone to talk about after I left or behind my back or, after many drinks, to my face. But I was still family no matter what. It always started off nice enough, but after a few hours and more than a few drinks, the scabs came off old hurts; disagreement became increasingly naked and feelings became tender targets. The family would say mean things to me, some of those things I wrote down in my notebook. Someone in the family would say, "Oh Lisa, you know they don't really mean it," or "You should think about what they said." I heard that very often.

But if an outsider even looked at me wrong, they had the whole family to deal with. I often saw loser boyfriends or loser girlfriends taken into the yard, out of my earshot, and given a stern, finger shaking and talking to. I was, after all, one of the family.

As November approached, I looked forward with feelings as confused as a marble cake. The swirls of chocolate and vanilla were dread and fondness.

I half-heartedly invited Dana and Alyssa but was a bit relieved when Dana declined. For years, the Artist Orphan Feast had been held for artist and dealers who happened to be in Atlanta over the holidays. Many artists and their dealers travel over the Thanksgiving holidays; it was often their busiest time of year. I arrived in LA on Tuesday and rented a car and a hotel room not two miles from Bridget's, the site of the confab. That was the right distance away from the confab to give me a little distance between me and my wacko extended family. Enough to preserve my sanity but close enough to be part of them when I wanted to.

Now, sitting in my hotel room, I missed Dana so much. We had been together almost every weekend. Now, we weren't just apart. We were on different ends of the continent.

After I relaxed a bit and fortified myself with a glass of wine, I called Bridget.

"I'm in. Okay if I come over now?" I asked. "Can I pick up anything?" She asked me to pick up dinner from the Thai restaurant in about half an hour where she would place an order.

Take-out; that was great. That meant a quiet evening at home; just Bridget, Scott, and Keela. *I wonder if anyone else is going to be there. I guess I'll find out.*

It was a quiet night, just the four of us. Bridget was relaxed and Keela was a wild child, who made me smile and laugh out loud. I thought, *Energy is what childhood is all about. Why walk when you can run? Why talk when you can laugh?*

Eventually, Keela laid down with her binky and five minutes later, she was out. Shortly thereafter, she was carried to bed. I decided it was time to go back to my hotel room and a comfy chair.

"Lisa." Bridget said putting her arm around me as we walked to the door. "Here is what I need, I need you to be on your best behavior, especially when everyone is here. Okay?"

"Moi? I'm always on my best behavior?" I feigned being shocked.

"Really." She pulled me toward her. "And I need you to babysit Keela tomorrow from about eleven to four."

"Really?" This time I was a little shocked "Sure, no problem. Happy to."

As the door closed behind me, I gave out a little squeal. *That's a first*, I thought. *I am being trusted with Keela for a whole day.* I floated all the way down the driveway to my car at the curb. "Wow," was all I could say when I got behind the wheel. *Wait 'til Dana hears about this*, I thought as I pulled out my cell phone.

***

I arrived at the appointed time. I was given my instructions and left alone with Keela.

I made her a lunch of mac and cheese. *What is it with mac and cheese? Ninety percent of all the mac and cheese in the world must be consumed by kids under twelve*, I thought as I prepared the meal. After lunch, we went to the kid's park by the beach where I was certain I had more fun than she did.

Back home, at about three o'clock, I got Keela her snack of choice, goldfish and bananas. Just as I sat her down at the table, I heard the front door open.

"Bridget?" I called out, thinking she had come home early.

"No." Ashley's voice answered.

"Oh shit," I said under my breath.

Ashley entered the room and said, "Keela baby! Hi, sweetie! What are you eating? That's not good for you!" She admonished, reached for the child's plate, trying to take it away.

209

Instantly, my hand came down on the edge of the plate. "Leave it," I said coolly. "Back off."

"What are you doing here?" I demanded.

"Just here to see my favorite granddaughter," Ashley said, "as a matter of fact."

It was a chilly half hour 'til Ashley discovered that one, it was only us in the house; there was no one else around to hear her put me down. And two, Keela liked her goldfish and bananas.

Ashley tried to make nice, well...as nice as Ashley could be toward me. Finally, she decided to leave. At the door, she said, "Lisa, you're looking good, I like that dress on you."

No answer came from my stony lips as I shut the door firmly behind her.

***

Thanksgiving morning I snuggled up in my comfy chair, dressed only in my T-shirt and panties. I took out my notebook and looking at I said as I opened it, "It's going to be one hell of a day. What do you have to tell me?" I began by reading the first few things I had written on the first day. I was reminded that I was told and accepted that I was disgusting. Also, I had written that I had to someday go back to that person and reject that.

I sat thinking about that. *It was time to confront that person from long ago.* I stood and ducked out of my T-shirt and slid out of my panties. In front of the bathroom, I stopped and looked at my naked self in the full length mirror, looking myself up and down, front and back. It wasn't long before I saw a glimpse of that person from long ago looking back at me in the mirror. I shook my finger at that person and said aloud, "You called me disgusting! I reject that. I'm not disgusting! I am now finally just as God meant me to be. I am a damn good-looking woman. A lady.

Good inside and out. So you will never ever say that..that word, to me again!" Turning away, I said over my shoulder, "Someone even calls me beautiful!"

With that out of my way, I showered and did my makeup. I dressed in a sassy red leather mini skirt to show off my legs and a low cut red blouse to show off my store-bought tits. I, of course, finished the ensemble off with as high a pair of red stilettos as I could find; if they had been a half inch higher, and I couldn't have possibly walked in them.

It was still early, and I needed to get back to my notebook. I reviewed every page with pen in hand. Here and there, I would underline a word or draw an arrow. An hour or so later, the notebook went back to its resting place in my purse.

I called Bridget to find out if there was anything I could pick up. "Oh God. I'm so glad you called," she said as she proceeded to give me a list.

***

Arriving at Von's Supermarket, I noted a sign on the door, *Closed at Noon for Thanksgiving.* It was only about ten, but the place was packed with last-minute shoppers. But the shopping went surprisingly fast, and I was back in my car just forty-five minutes later.

I parked in the driveway, as close to the house as possible; popped the trunk and gathered up myself and a few bags, leaving the trunk open. With some difficulty, I rang the doorbell. Not waiting, I tried the door; it swung open, putting me face-to-face with my ex-brother-in-law. Apparently the party had already started. Quickly he reached for my bags to relieve me of them.

"Wow! Lisa, you look great," he said. "Sean!," He shouted toward the living room. "Come on your mom's here. There's more bags."

My son greeted me with a kiss on the cheek as he passed by me, heading toward my car outside and said, "Barbara is in the living room. Go say hi." At the car, collecting bags, he yelled back to no one in particular, "Jesus! Didn't we have enough food already?"

I put my purse down and turned to go back out. "I got them," Mark, my other ex-brother-in-law, said as he too gave me a kiss on the cheek. *God, it's great to be a woman,* I thought to myself.

We went through the usual greeting ritual of, "Hi, It's been so long! You look great."

And, "Oh thanks. You're looking wonderful."

"I'd like you to meet..."

"Nice meeting you..." etc., blah blah blah.

Until finally, I worked my way to Barbara. "So, you're my son's new woman?" I asked.

"Hi, Lisa," Barbara said as she stood up and smiled. "Sean told me all about you. And, yes, we have been going out for over seven months." Smiling warmly she greeted me with a kiss on the cheek. "I'm not the new woman anymore," she said whispering in my ear "I'm his last girlfriend...ever."

I stood back and looked her up and down. "Your just what he needs" I said and then I leaned in and confidentially whispered in her ear, "He's a lot of work."

She whispered back "I can handle him."

I kissed her on the cheek and whispered "If you need any help, let me know. I'm on your side."

"Sean, she's gorgeous," I called back to my son. "She's a keeper!" I said as Barbara and I winked at each other.

"Told ya!," Sean responded.

I entered the kitchen to help in any way I could. "Hi, sweetie," I said giving Bridget a kiss on the cheek. "What can I do?"

"Hi, Lisa," Jessie, my good ex, called out from her position at the sink. Turning around, she, looked me up and down. "You're looking sexy," she said dramatically rolling her eyes.

"What?" I said, reading her mind, knowing she really meant slutty.

"Nothing." That meant really slutty, but I'm not going to say anything, she retorted.

"Let me guess. Skirt is too short and too much cleavage?" I said. I knew Jessie so well.

"No, no. Dress how you're most comfortable," she said. "But, are those pumps really that comfortable?"

"I'll take that as, 'Lisa, you look gorgeous.'" as I gave Jessie a kiss on the cheek then received one in return.

"Hi, Lisa," I heard Ashley say.

"Hi, Ashley," I said as I turned to wash and slice up the strawberries.

The next words out of her mouth were, "New boob job?"

I turned, hip out, with my hand on my waist, leaning a little forward, and jutted my chest out, showing as much cleavage as I could possibly muster. "No. Ashley. I bought them quite a while ago. Do you like them?" *Don't let her get the best of me*, I thought.

"Ashley, do something or get out of the kitchen." Bridget said, breaking the awkward scene up.

"Kind of rude," Jessie said to me, quietly.

"Like you're so nice to me," I responded laughing lightly.

"When we were married, they weren't that big." She said, reaching up and squeezing my right breast. "Or that firm."

"For sure." I laughed.

Keeping in mind what I had learned, I cruised through the day, laughing, chatting, accepting, and rejecting. "No, it's not that way," I said and, "Sure I love it." But always keeping happy. Several run-ins with Ashley were easily handled. And the few just plain mean remarks were quickly dealt with.

Wine glasses were filled and refilled. Conversations wandered from room to room and out to the patio or front porch and back again. Slowly the crowd migrated toward the dining table.

The table was set, and everyone was finding our places. When my cell phone that was sitting next to me on the table rang. I had been hoping that Dana would call and let me know how the Artist Orphan Feast was going. Quickly, I answered the call. "Dana honey, I miss you so much! I wish you and Alyssa were here," I said.

"Wish granted! Look out the front window." He replied.

I nearly knocked my chair over, rushing to the window. Standing on the sidewalk was Dana, waving with cell phone in and hand, next to him was Alyssa.

I let out a squeal and waved them toward the front door. "They're here!" I called out excitedly to the others as I rushed to the front door and opened it. Dana's embraced me and delivered a long kiss as Alyssa's arms found me and hugged me tightly too.

"Hi, beautiful," Dana said. "Alyssa and I discussed it last night. It didn't feel right without you. We need to be with you today. I need to be with you all the time."

During the excitement, most of the family had left the table and formed a crowd between us and the living room.

"Family," I said. "I would like you to meet Alyssa and Dana."

My daughter, Bridget made her way through the crowd to stand in front of Dana where she looked him for a few seconds that felt like minutes. Finally, she threw open her arms and said, "Welcome."

We began to make our way to the table, with Bridget ordering, "Set two more places," to no one in particular but expecting it to be obeyed nonetheless.

Ashely, who had remained seated during the excitement with the older people spouted off to them, "I don't know who they are. They just show up. No warning Kind of rude, I think."

Instantly, Bridget's finger shot into the air toward Ashley's face. "Shut up, Ashley!" She admonished, having none of it.

Ashley's mouth snapped shut in surprise.

"Mom's friends are our friends, and I've got a feeling they are going to be family from now on."

My body vibrated, as it searched for new places to pack in my new-found happiness. Through prisms of tears in my eyes, I could only say, "Thank you, daughter."

WE MEET AGAIN

Chapter 23

Mother Ocean waited patiently for the return of her sun to her bosom. Bridget, Scott, Dana, and I sat on a blanket on the beach, sipping wine out of nondescript travel cups.

The Sunday evening air was warm and still. Keela had found a new best friend in Alyssa, and Alyssa treated her like her new little sister. The girls frolicked in the little waves in the wet sand, between us and the setting sun. We watched as they bent over studying something they had found in the sand, and reached out with their fingers here and there to try a little quick poke.

Bridget broke our companionable silence. "So, Lisa, you're going back to Chicago tomorrow?"

"Yes, unfortunately," I answered as I leaned against Dana.

"And Dana, you and Alyssa are going back to Atlanta tomorrow?"

"That's right," Dana said, patting my thigh.

"So how is it exactly that you're going to make this relationship work?" Bridget asked.

"We see each other almost every week, somewhere. It's like a traveling circus," Dana explained.

"And how long do you think you can keep that up?" Bridget continued.

Dana and I looked at each other and he patted my thigh again as we looked out to sea, not answering her question.

We sat quite in our own thoughts, enjoying the gray and white Mother Ocean welcoming her orange and red sun at the end of the day as Alyssa and Keela came running back up the beach; dropping to their knees as they planted themselves in front of us; joining us as we all enjoyed the final rays of the sun kissing Mother Ocean's waves good night.

***

The three of us returned for Christmas, planning on spending the week. The family had, by then, assimilated Dana and Alyssa and, with some, reluctance me.

Christmas day, would be at Jessie's house. Christmas morning, Bridget, Scott, Keela, Sean, Barbara, Dana, Alyssa, and I gathered around Bridget's tree to enjoy our Christmas morning as Scott and Bridget handed out the gifts. Yards, if not miles, of Christmas wrapping paper, ribbons, and bows were ripped apart and scattered around the living room.

Everyone had managed to build a pile of presents next to our chairs except for Keela. Hers gifts were spread all over the room; as soon as she would open a present, she would squeal, play with it for maybe thirty seconds, and then leave it sitting where it was; moving on to open the next present.

After about a hurried half hour, the excitement of the morning began to calm. Keela sat playing with her dolls and toy cars. And the rest of us settled in with our eggnog, smiling and chatting.

"Oh, I almost forgot," Dana said reaching into his pocket to retrieve a small square present. "Here, Lisa, this is for you," he said holding the box out toward me.

The size and timing suggested something very special. I unwrapped it to find a small blue jewelry box, the size rings came in. I held my breath as my heart began to pound out of my chest while I held the tiny box in the middle of my hand and stared at it. Time was frozen.

Finally, Dana reached over to open it. "Will you marry me," Dana asked, showing me a beautiful diamond ring.

"Of course! Oh yes! Yes! Yes!" I replied breathlessly as I embraced him and we kissed and Dana slipped the ring on my finger; it was a perfect fit.

Everyone cheered and gathered around us to see the ring and congratulate us. Bridget became a serial hugger and kisser, starting with Dana, Alyssa, Scott, Keela, Sean, Barbara, and finally, me. "I'm so happy," Bridget said. "God, I feel like your mom. Not your daughter."

I called Paula as soon as possible. When she heard the news she screamed and tole me how happy she was for us. In the background her husband Dave said, "I told you so."

A little while later Alyssa, Dana, and I returned to our hotel rooms to change into our party clothes for the Christmas party. An hour later, we were ready and on our way over to Jessie's house for the family Christmas party.

***

I had warned Bridget not to tell anybody about the engagement, it was something I wanted to do; I wanted to see the expressions on everyone's faces. By the time we got there, Bridget and the rest of the family had arrived, including Ashley.

We walked in and greeted everyone with hugs, but no one had noticed my ring. Approaching Jessie, I held up my left hand and said, "What's that? There." With my hand directly in front of her face Jessie could not help but looked at my hand. "Oh my God, you're getting married again!" She exclaimed as she grabbed my hand to examine the ring and then lifted it up to show everyone.

"When?" Jessie asked.

"We haven't planned the wedding yet. I just got proposed to this morning!" I replied, smiling widely.

Over the next few hours everyone came by to wish us luck and ensure that they received invitations to the wedding. Even Ashley kissed me on the cheek and congratulated me, leaving me waiting for the zinger that never came.

***

During the next few days, as a group, we made plans. Bridget and I called family and friends to make the grand announcement and worked on possibilities for the wedding date.

Both Bridget and Jessie offered their houses up for the reception or a party.

"No, but thank you so much. I know where we want our wedding, just not when," I informed them. "It's going to be on the beach in Hawaii, on the sand near our bench. The reception can be at the hotel pool area."

"Great! We're in. If we're going that far. We need to do some serious timing. We probably need to do it during some kind of school break. So we need to keep that in mind as we plan the date," said Bridget, who was always the practical one.

***

The day before we left for home, Bridget decided to take me into a wedding dress shop.

As we entered the dress shop, a sales agent approached her asking, "What can I do for you?"

"Nothing, but my Mom here is going to need a wedding dress," she said, pointing to me.

We sipped champagne as we browsed through rack after rack of wedding dresses.

"No, no, no, it's got to be white, Mom," Bridget instructed me.

"Okay, but not long," I pleaded.

"Not mini either, I don't care if you got great legs" Bridget ordered.

Well, into our second bottle of champagne and at about the fifth try-on, we finally settled on a dress we both liked. White and just above the knee. It was satin, overlaid with white lace. Bridget's one concession was that it showed cleavage. The argument went this way:

"I paid a lot for these babies, they got to breathe."

"Breathe, yes but they are hyperventilating!"

"Please, I'll wear pearls!" I begged.

"Okay, I do love the dress." Bridget acquiesced.

She was happy. I was happy. The world was happy.

Bridget surprised me when we went to pay for the dress, by insisting on paying for it. "I'll pick it up when it's ready." She said, insisting on several alterations.

We toasted our victory and Bridget gave me a kiss and a hug. "You'll be a beautiful bride, Mom," she said.

***

A few months later, we had worked out the living and business arrangements. Paula was going to take a bigger piece of the business and more responsibility. Alyssa, who was quite good at the art business, was also going to get a big piece of the business and, with it, more responsibility. Dana and I were not completely divorcing ourselves from our businesses, just delegating more responsibility to give us more time together.

We decided to live in my house in Chicago in the spring and summer, and Dana's house in the fall and winter; with Thanksgiving and Christmas spent in LA. Our wedding would be in the spring, during Easter break.

I called Porter in Hawaii for advice. I told him all about the planed wedding and when it would be. "Porter, you know everything and everybody. Who can I trust to make the arrangements?" I asked. "I need somebody on the ground there."

"Lisa, may I? Please allow me to make the arrangements?" Porter offered sincerely.

"I was hoping you would say that! You're my favorite and most trusted friend in Hawaii. I know you will do a grand job." I said, relieved that he offered. "Thank you!"

***

Our wedding day proved to be quite a gathering: Bridget and her family; Sean and Barbara, of course; Jessie, and even Ashley; and many other friends and relatives had assembled for our big day. I don't know how he did it, but Porter even arranged to have the governor and his guards and the congressman in attendance; even Paul the attorney was there, and of course, Keri, who was a bride's maid along with Bridget, Alyssa, and Barbara.

Our barefoot wedding on the sand was scheduled so that our vows would be exchanged just before sunset. Everyone walked down to the beach barefooted, and then back to the hotel pool for our reception party. It was a beautiful night.

***

The next morning, I slipped out of bed around 4:00 a.m. I pulled on a longer, new T-shirt and panties and then leaned in to give Dana a kiss on the lips. With eyes still closed, Dana pointed toward the dresser. "You'll find champagne and a champagne flute over there."

"Thanks, honey."

"No problem, beautiful."

Barefoot, I walked across the lobby and out onto the sand toward the dark ocean. A slight breeze carried the scent ocean toward me, gently filling my nose and mouth and blowing my hair gently back from my face. I popped the cork; sending it flying into Mother Ocean who splashed back her "thanks."

I slowly walked the water's edge, sipping my champagne and letting the waves lick my toes and lower legs.

Once again, I found myself sitting in the sand at the water's edge, knees tucked under my chin. "Aloha, myself," I said.

"Aloha, myself." I answered as I sat, waiting for myself to say something.

"Pretty weird trip!" I finally said to myself, trying to remember life before meeting myself on that very same beach.

Looking into myself, I realize I can remember every detail of meeting myself that morning, not so long ago.

Again, myself and I sat on beach, anticipating the arrival of the sun, sipping my champagne.

"So what did you learn?" Myself asked me.

"That I am responsible for so much more than my own happiness."

THE END

Continue reading for a free preview of
Red's Revenge
Book 1, in the *The Love and Revenge* series.

JANE B. LEE

RED'S
REVENGE

Red's Revenge

Love and Revenge Series

Book 1

Jane B. Lee

CHAPTER 1

Godzilla Meets Stump

"Hey, Stump," Ron called out as he and Moses ran Gina down. It had not taken long after Ron got out of prison to find Gina.

"Hey, Stump. Wait up," he called to Gina.

Ron and Moses quickly backed twelve-year-old Gina up against a chain-link fence.

"You got me two years in the slammer," Ron slapped Gina across the face, "You should have never called the cops." Ron angrily spat out the words. Slapping her across the face again and again, he grabbed her by the throat, lifting her onto her toes. He then ripped open her blouse and pulled up her skirt.

The sudden pain of his little finger breaking caused him to release his prisoner. Turning, he faced a very tall, thin twelve-year-old Dana.

"What the fuck?" He yelled.

Moses grabbed Dana by her hair. Dana's well-placed stomp broke three critical bones. He quickly lost the use of his left foot as he let Dana's hair go with a loud, "Fuck!"

Gina had fallen to the ground when Ron turned to take a swing at Dana; she easily avoided the blow. Before Ron could complete the swing, he felt his sixth rib on his right-side break.

Moses pulled his gun from the back of his pants. Dana kicked in his right knee, breaking it at the joint. His 9mm automatic flew across the street as he hit the ground. He was not going to stand for quite a while.

Ron tried to kick Dana. She pushed his leg even higher, dropping him on his back. As he hit the ground, Dana dropped a knee in his chest, breaking his ninth rib.

With both men down, Dana turned to help Gina up off the ground. Seeing Gina's eyes grow wide, Dana quickly pivoted to react to Ron pointing a gun at her head. She turned the gun backward toward the ground, breaking more of Ron's fingers in the process. She then threw a palm at his jaw, breaking it, and followed up with a blow to the side of Ron's head; his eyes rolled back as he hit the ground.

With the men down, Dana turned to Gina, who was still leaning against the fence, her blouse torn open, pulling her blouse over her small chest. Dana asked, "Are you okay? You're bleeding," Dana saw blood coming out of her nose and lip.

"No. No, I'm okay," Gina's eyes, which were rolling around in her head, told Dana a different story.

"I'm Dana. They call me Godzilla at school, and you're Stump, right?" Dana said, putting her arm around Gina's shoulders. She walked her down the street, turning their backs on the two men lying on the sidewalk. "So, Stump, what's your real name?" Dana asked calmly.

"Gina," she said, looking up at her protector.

"I've seen you around the school." Dana was talking to her in a calming voice as if nothing had happened. Gina's whole body was still trembling. As they rounded the corner two blocks down the street, they heard sirens announcing the arrival of the police.

"There they are," the crossing guard announced, pointing the police in the direction of the fight. The police approached the men with drawn guns. Ron was lying on his back on the sidewalk, out cold with his gun still in his hand. Moses was crawling across the street.

Standing over Moses, the officer asked, "Where are you going, buddy?"

"To get my gun and shoot that fucking kid who did this to me," was Moses's answer.

"No worries. I'll get it." The officer said with a chuckle. He had never got a confession so fast.

***

"Where do you live, Gina?" Dana asked as they walked along. "Over off Piedmont. Those apartments. You know."

"Oh. That's like ten blocks. My house is just over a few blocks. Let's go there and fix you up." Dana guided her toward her house.

Eve was leaving home for her shift at the hospital when she saw the girls walking up the sidewalk. The minute she saw the way her daughter was protecting the little girl, she knew something was very wrong. When she noticed the torn blouse and blood on the little girl's face, Eve rushed to meet them on the sidewalk. "What happened?"

"Mom, this is Gina. She goes to my school." Eve had gotten down on one knee and was examining Gina's bloody lip and nose. The wounds had stopped bleeding, but there was plenty of dried blood on her face. The bruises on her face and neck were just starting to get an ugly purple color. Eve then stopped to look at Dana and do a quick inspection. She didn't expect to see any blood or bruises.

"Come with me, honey," Eve said, taking Gina by the hand. "We'll fix you up.". As they started walking toward the house, Eve ordered, "Dana, talk!"

Dana began to tell her story as they entered the house. With Gina in the middle, they headed to the kitchen. "I was coming home from school when I saw these two men. One was beating Gina up," Dana started.

Gina was quiet as Eve sat her in a chair and carefully wiped the blood from her face with a wet towel. Eve checked carefully checked Gina's eyes, ears, and nose. Looking at the bruising on her throat, she stopped Dana and asked Gina a few questions. Eve was listening to her voice and breathing to determine if there was any other damage.

"Go on, Dana. Describe what happened," Eve said, as Dana continued her description, Eve opened the refrigerator door, taking out an ever-present ice pack used for moves gone wrong on the martial arts mat outback. She put the ice pack on the side of Gina's bruised face. "Honey, hold this. It will keep the swelling down. OK, Dana, stay with Gina. I'll get her a new blouse," Eve said, on the way upstairs, she stopped and called the police, asking that they bring an EMS with them. Then a quick call to the hospital, telling her supervisor she had a family emergency and wouldn't be in today. Back with the girls, Eve explained that the police had to talk with them.

"Everything will be alright. Just tell the truth. Also, I asked for a nurse to give you a check-up," Eve was looking at Gina. "Gina, I'm a nurse. So, when I tell you that there is no damage and you will heal, you know I'm telling you the truth."

Gina nodded in agreement. "Gina, I need to call your mom."

"I live with my aunt. She's a flight attendant. She won't be home 'til the day after tomorrow. I can't always call her. My sitter won't be at my house 'til five," Gina explained.

"We should call the sitter then," Eve said.

"Her name is Alice, and she's new. I don't know her number," Gina answered.

"Okay, what's your phone number? We'll call your sitter at five." Eve wrote down the number as Gina called it out.

Dana and Gina were still sitting in the kitchen when a plainclothes detective, a uniformed officer, and the EMS nurse showed up at the door.

Eve led everyone into the kitchen. The detective directed the nurse to check out Gina and document her wounds.

Stepping around the men, she noticed Eve, "Oh, Hi, Eve. These your kids?"

"Just the tall one, Susan. I think Gina, the shorter one, doesn't have any long-term trauma. Other than bruises and a split lip. But you make sure," Eve said.

"So, you're a doctor?" The detective asked Eve.

"No, just a nurse. Susan and I work out of the same hospital... You're Detective Lawrence," Eve said, recognizing him, "You got shot in the left leg, maybe two years ago. I took care of you at the hospital."

The detective gave Eve a half-smile and shrugged. He had been too doped up to remember. "Okay, where is the guy who beat up those other guys? The ones we found on the sidewalk, over near the high school?" He asked.

"Oh, that was me," Dana said, her eyes wide.

"No, the tall one who beat up the bad guys?" The detective asked again.

"That was me," Dana stood up, showing off her five-foot eight-inch, still growing thin frame.

Detective Lawrence was shaking his head. He began again. "The crossing guard saw a tall kid beating up those bad guys. So, who was it?"

"That was Dana," Gina said, grabbing Dana's arm.

"Come on. Who was it?" The detective asked again, pointing his finger at Gina.

"I believe that was my daughter, Dana," Eve stepped in. "She's well capable of that."

"Come on; they had guns. Who was it?" The detective said, looking around.

"Dana, explain to the detective, please, what you did, move by move," Eve said to Dana.

Dana put her hands up in a Karate attack pose, "No, Dana." Eve said, "Tell in detail. Do not demonstrate. Now sit down, please."

"Well, I was across the street when I saw this guy slapping Gina really hard," Dana started.

"Can you describe him? Was his partner with the guy attacking Gina?"

The nurse had finished up with Gina. She handed a report on a clipboard to the detective, who signed it. The nurse took off the top copy and gave it to him.

"It is just like you said, Eve. There's nothing that won't heal. See you at the hospital." The nurse gathered her things and made her way out the door.

"Okay, where were we?" Detective Lawrence folded the report and put it in his pocket.

Dana went on to describe, move by move, what she did and what the bad guys did. A lot of her descriptions used martial arts terms.

Eve would come in and give a more generic description of her moves. After a few more questions, Detective Lawrence was finally convinced. He had to believe the unbelievable. This young girl took on two dangerous men on purpose and beat the hell out of them.

"Okay, I guess you're the man. Sorry, you're what? A tough, dangerous little girl," the detective said, looking for a description.

"They call me Godzilla at school because I'm so tall," Dana said. "I guess now I'll never live that name down."

"They call me Stump because I'm so short," Gina said, extending her hand to shake the detectives.

"Well, I'm delighted to meet you, brave girls." Detective Lawrence said. "If I ever need help, I'll give you a call."

The girls giggled.

"No, really," he said with his eyes wide open. The girls giggled again.

The detective stood, wrapping up his most unbelievable interview ever. Under his breath, he said, "They're never going to believe this at the station house."

"Detective, would it be okay if Gina stays with us tonight?" Eve asked.

"Yes, can she, Mom?" Dana asked.

"Can I stay with Dana?" Gina asked Eve, taking Dana's arm.

"That would be great," the detective said. "I'll send a car around to talk to the sitter. But I'm sure it will be okay. I guess the sitter can tell us how and when we can contact your aunt."

"Can I call my husband now?" Eve asked.

"Sure, Mind if I finish up a few notes before I go. I might have another question or two."

Christopher was home in less than fifteen minutes. Detective Lawrence met Christopher outside on the sidewalk.

"You have an amazing and brave little girl there. Have her describe how she took down two thugs with guns. She probably saved Gina from rape and death. Amazing." Shaking Christopher's hand, the detective instructed the other patrol car to wait here and to go to Gina's house around five, telling them, "Make sure they're not disturbed." Signaling the uniform officer that they were leaving, the detective handed Christopher his card. "Call me anytime."

As the detective and the uniformed officer got into their patrol car, the detective said, "I hope the press goes easy on them."

They didn't.

Dana met her dad at the door. She got a great big hug. "Are you okay?" He asked and then turned to Eve. "She's okay, right?"

"Yes. And this is Gina," Eve waved her hand toward Gina.

Christopher, with his arm still around Dana, led them all into the library. Eve poured two glasses of wine and handed one to Christopher before taking her seat.

"Okay, Dana, what happened?" Christopher asked, looking at Dana and Gina on the sofa.

Before Dana could get beyond, "I was across the street," Lars came crashing in.

"What happened?" Lars was confused. "That cop out there gave me the third degree, patted me down, and asked for my driver's license."

"Lars, this is Gina. Gina, this is my son Lars. Lars, Gina's going to be our house guest tonight." Eve said.

"Hi, Lars," Gina said. Lars gave her a little wave.

"Okay, Dana. Start over," Christopher said as Lars took his seat.

Almost an hour later, Dana finished up by saying, "I don't see I had a choice."

Eve had been going back and forth, preparing dinner. Before Christopher could voice his opinion, Eve announced, "Dinner's on the table. Come on."

At the table, Christopher said, "I don't see you had much choice, either." He took a big spoon of rice and passed the bowl on, "But if there ever is a next time, please look for alternatives," He picked out a piece of chicken from the plate on the table. "It could have turned out much worse."

With a little smile, Eve said, "You did good, Dana."

***

Dana dressed Gina in one of her nighties. It fell off her shoulders. She then gave her an old t-shirt. It came to Gina's knees. Gina joined Dana in her bed. Dana fell asleep almost as soon as her head hit the pillow. Gina looked at the back of Dana's head, put her arm on Dana's shoulder, and fell into a quiet sleep.

***

"Who the hell is that at this time in the morning," Lars looked over at the clock. It was just after six am. He threw off his covers. He was wearing just his flannel pajama bottoms, barefoot and bare-chested. He stomped his way to the front door, opening the door, to a mic shoved in his face and a foot in the door.

"I'm Tim Slaid. This is NBC, can you..." Was all the reporter could get out before his mic went flying, and his wrist bent back as he was forced out the door.

"You shouldn't do that. You don't come into my home unless you're invited," Lars said, his attention drawn to the front yard. His mouth dropped open as he saw three cameras filming him, then a dozen people in the yard trampling down the hedges and flower beds, digging up the grass. Television trucks with three different logos were blocking the street.

Lars slammed the door. Putting his back up against the door and his eyes wide, he yelled, "Mom, Dad!" as he ran up the stairs. Bursting through their door, he found Christopher and Eve already awake from the commotion.

Lars stood there, just waving his hands and arms. Words were not coming out of his mouth. Pointing at the window, he squeaked, "news."

Christopher and Eve were looking out the window as Lars came in, "Shit. They're digging up the yard. Trampling the bushes and flower beds." Eve grabbed her robe and headed for the door.

"Hold on," a sleepy Christopher said, slowing Eve down. "First, go get Dana, and what's her name. We'll all meet in the hall."

Dana and Gina were still asleep when Eve entered. Dana was on her side, and Gina's arm was draped across her shoulder. "Girls, up," Eve ordered, shaking Dana's shoulder.

Two minutes later, they all gathered in the hall. Christopher had been looking out the window, summing up the situation.

"Okay, here's what we do. First, we all get dressed. I'll call the detective right now and find out what we should do and what we can or can't say." They just stood looking at him. "Move!" He ordered.

Ten minutes later, they were all gathered in the kitchen. Eve had started the coffee. Christopher came in just as the phone rang.

"This is NBC news. Can you—" Christopher hung up. The news called every thirty seconds or so until Christopher shouted into the phone, "Quit calling," Before he could hang up, he heard, "This is Detective Lawrence," The phone was already a few inches from his ear.

"Oh. Thank you. It's chaotic around here," Christopher said.

"So, I've been told. A patrol car is on its way. They'll back them out of your yard and have them park properly. Now, what?" The detective asked.

"What do we do? What do we say?" Christopher asked.

"Give it a half hour. We'll get everything in order. The press won't be easy on you." The detective was warming up. "Do not take the girls out there. Don't say anything about them. Don't answer any questions directly."

"They won't like that," Christopher pressed.

"I know," the detective said. "Just say please respect our privacy, da, da, da."

"Okay, we'll try. Anything else?"

"No. Those newsmen are experts at digging things out of you. Just don't give in." The detective had no other advice.

"Thanks." Christopher hung up and turned to the group and said, "So, here's what we do."

Thirty minutes later, Christopher, Eve, and Lars stepped in front of the cameras and mics at the end of the driveway near the sidewalk. Three newsmen shouted out the same question three different ways, all at once. Ten minutes later, Christopher, Eve, and Lars retreated into the house.

That day, the morning, noon, and evening news on every station had the same thing, just with a different newsman's name.

Tim Slaid said it best. "I'm Tim Slaid. This is your exclusive news." NBC had him standing in front of the Perssons' house. They then cut away to Lars, opening the door, tossing the mic away, and forcing Tim Slaid out the door. They then cut to a closeup of Lars standing open-mouthed in the doorway in only his pajama bottoms, his bare, muscular chest fully exposed.

After a short explanation about the twelve-year-old girl who took on the brutal bad guys and won, Tim Slaid finished with, "This is one family you don't want to fool with."

Red's Revenge

Book 1, in the *The Love and Revenge* series.

Available at Amazon and other retailers today!

ACKNOWLEDGMENTS

Paula Lehman—She followed along with me, reading chapter after chapter as I completed them. She not only gave me input but also encouragement.

Anita Moore of Cyber-Bytz.com—Book Formatter. Her perfect mind for words, sentences, paragraphs, and novels made all the difference in the world! Not to mention her patience with me. Thank you, friend.

Jay Lipscomb and Chandra Corley—My Beta readers. They showed me when and where I was off course.

Susan Helene Gotfried of westofmars.com—Her advice on content drove me in the right direction, plus all the other things she helped direct me with to become a better writer.

Humbert Glaffo at 99Designers—He designed an outstanding cover.

Robert Lewis at Southern Editing & Cover Design—He gave me fast and cost-effective editing.

Finally—All the bartenders who kept my wine glass full and gave me space to write.

Lightning Source UK Ltd.
Milton Keynes UK
UKHW011841010621
384770UK00001B/37